365 days of BLACK HISTORY

2002 Engagement Calendar

Catalog No. 202050

Published by Pomegranate Communications, Inc., Box 6099, Rohnert Park, California 94927

© 2001 IOKTS Productions

www.iokts.com

Available in Canada from Canadian Manda Group,
One Atlantic Avenue #105, Toronto, Ontario M6K 3E7, Canada

Available in the U.K. and mainland Europe from Pomegranate Europe Ltd.,
Fullbridge House, Fullbridge, Maldon, Essex CM9 4LE, England

Available in Australia from Hardie Grant Books,
12 Claremont Street, South Yarra, Victoria 3141

Available in New Zealand from Randy Horwood Ltd., P.O. Box 32-077, Devonport, Auckland

Available in Asia (including the Middle East), Africa, and Latin America from
Pomegranate International Sales, 113 Babcombe Drive, Thornhill, Ontario L3T 1M9, Canada

Several photographs in this edition of *365 Days of Black History* were taken by the Philadelphia photographer John Mosley and were acquired through the courtesy of Charles L. Blockson, curator of the Charles L. Blockson African-American Collection, Temple University.

Pomegranate also publishes the 2002 calendars *African American Art, Black Ball: The Negro Baseball Leagues, African Kings, African Masks, African Textiles,* and *Women of the African Ark,* as well as many other calendars in several formats. Our products and publications include books, posters, postcards and books of postcards, notecards and boxed notecard sets, magnets, mousepads, Knowledge Cards™, appointment books and journals, address books, screen savers, and bookmarks. For more information or to place an order, please contact Pomegranate Communications, Inc.: 800-227-1428; www.pomegranate.com

Front cover image:
Jeanne Walker Rorex
At Day's End, 1991
Acrylic on canvas, 18 x 12 in.

Cover design by Lisa Reid

All astronomical data supplied in this calendar are expressed in Greenwich Mean Time (GMT). Moon phases and American, Canadian, and U.K. holidays are noted.

● NEW MOON ◗ FIRST QUARTER ○ FULL MOON ◗ LAST QUARTER

2002

january

s	m	t	w	t	f	s
		1	2	3	4	5
6	7	8	9	10	11	12
13	14	15	16	17	18	19
20	21	22	23	24	25	26
27	28	29	30	31		

february

s	m	t	w	t	f	s
					1	2
3	4	5	6	7	8	9
10	11	12	13	14	15	16
17	18	19	20	21	22	23
24	25	26	27	28		

march

s	m	t	w	t	f	s
					1	2
3	4	5	6	7	8	9
10	11	12	13	14	15	16
17	18	19	20	21	22	23
24	25	26	27	28	29	30
31						

april

s	m	t	w	t	f	s
	1	2	3	4	5	6
7	8	9	10	11	12	13
14	15	16	17	18	19	20
21	22	23	24	25	26	27
28	29	30				

may

s	m	t	w	t	f	s
			1	2	3	4
5	6	7	8	9	10	11
12	13	14	15	16	17	18
19	20	21	22	23	24	25
26	27	28	29	30	31	

june

s	m	t	w	t	f	s
						1
2	3	4	5	6	7	8
9	10	11	12	13	14	15
16	17	18	19	20	21	22
23	24	25	26	27	28	29
30						

july

s	m	t	w	t	f	s
	1	2	3	4	5	6
7	8	9	10	11	12	13
14	15	16	17	18	19	20
21	22	23	24	25	26	27
28	29	30	31			

august

s	m	t	w	t	f	s
				1	2	3
4	5	6	7	8	9	10
11	12	13	14	15	16	17
18	19	20	21	22	23	24
25	26	27	28	29	30	31

september

s	m	t	w	t	f	s
1	2	3	4	5	6	7
8	9	10	11	12	13	14
15	16	17	18	19	20	21
22	23	24	25	26	27	28
29	30					

october

s	m	t	w	t	f	s
		1	2	3	4	5
6	7	8	9	10	11	12
13	14	15	16	17	18	19
20	21	22	23	24	25	26
27	28	29	30	31		

november

s	m	t	w	t	f	s
					1	2
3	4	5	6	7	8	9
10	11	12	13	14	15	16
17	18	19	20	21	22	23
24	25	26	27	28	29	30

december

s	m	t	w	t	f	s
1	2	3	4	5	6	7
8	9	10	11	12	13	14
15	16	17	18	19	20	21
22	23	24	25	26	27	28
29	30	31				

365 days of BLACK HISTORY

IOKTS Productions ("I Only Know The Story") is dedicated to the research of documented history for the purpose of exhibiting the contributions of black people from all cultures, races, and geographic locations. Through our work we strive to promote awareness, knowledge, and understanding among all people while furthering pride, dignity, and inspiration in those who identify directly with this heritage.

For more information, e-mail us at iokts@iokts.com or contact:

Mr. G. Theodore Catherine

IOKTS Productions

7007 Carroll Avenue, Suite 2

Takoma Park, MD 20912

301-270-1920

The majority of the photographs in this calendar are reproduced by courtesy of Charles Blockson, African American Collection, Temple University; the National Archive; and the Library of Congress. Our thanks to these archives, and to the artists and other contributors to this edition of *365 Days of Black History*.

RENEE T. LACHMAN

A practicing artist for thirty years, a resident of Takoma Park, Maryland, and a member of the Takoma Artists' Guild, Renee Lachman has taught art to kids in Takoma, at the University of Maryland's Art and Learning Center, and at the Art League for Kids in Alexandria, Virginia. Lachman credits her four-year-old daughter for showing her how much fun it is to work with children. Her current focus is on pursuing exhibitions and teaching positions.

Lachman observes of her painting *Fitting*: "Photos I'd taken at the Takoma Farmers' Market formed a loose association in my mind with Caribbean vendors, whom I'd observed during several visits to the islands. The Caribbean land- and seascape helped shape my artistic sensibility. You can see this in my paintings of fruits and vegetables, the richly patterned clothing and the give-and-take of black figures. The islands and their people have touched my heart; I hope it shows in my work."

The City of Takoma Park recently commissioned Lachman to paint several city scenes on the outside wall of a local market. A selection committee member said Lachman was chosen "because her themes were quintessential Takoma Park."

FITTING, 1998
Porcelain on tile, 6 x 8 in.
Photograph courtesy Renee T. Lachman

s	m	t	w	t	f	s
		1	2	3	4	5
6	7	8	9	10	11	12
13	14	15	16	17	18	19
20	21	22	23	24	25	26
27	28	29	30	31		

JANUARY

Kuumba (Creativity)
To do as much as we can, in whatever way we can, to leave our community more beautiful and beneficial than it was when we inherited it.

monday 31 365

NEW YEAR'S DAY
Kwanzaa ends
Imani (Faith)
To believe with all our hearts in our people, our parents, our teachers, our leaders, and the righteousness and victory of our struggle.

tuesday 1 1

BANK HOLIDAY (SCOTLAND)
1898: Sadie Tanner Mossell Alexander, first African American to earn a Ph.D. in economics, is born in Philadelphia, Pa.

wednesday 2 2

1621: William Tucker is the first African American to be born in America.

thursday 3 3

1920: Andrew "Rube" Foster organizes the first black baseball league, the Negro National League.

friday 4 4

1911: Kappa Alpha Psi Fraternity is chartered as a national organization.

saturday 5 5

1993: Jazz trumpeter John Birks "Dizzy" Gillespie dies.

sunday 6 6

DR. GEORGE R. CARRUTHERS

Inventor George Carruthers was born in Cincinnati, Ohio, in 1939. As a child he developed a keen interest in astronomy and space exploration.

Dr. Carruthers received his B.S. degree in 1961, his M.S. in 1962, and his Ph.D (in aeronautics and astronautical engineering) in 1964. Now senior astrophysicist at the Naval Research Laboratory, Dr. Carruthers is a quiet professional whose research projects have substantially contributed to the advancement of America's space program. In 1970 he proposed to NASA to set up an ultraviolet camera on the surface of the moon, to look back at the earth's atmosphere and to observe celestial bodies. With the camera he designed, NASA astronauts on *Apollo 16* saw for the first time that the hydrogen gas atmosphere of the earth extends many thousands of miles into deep space. Carruthers also developed a rocket-borne telescope to photograph ultraviolet star radiation, as well as the equipment used to analyze photo images from the telescope. In recognition of his work, Dr. Carruthers has received awards from NASA and other agencies.

Photograph courtesy NASA

s	m	t	w	t	f	s
		1	2	3	4	5
6	7	8	9	10	11	12
13	14	15	16	17	18	19
20	21	22	23	24	25	26
27	28	29	30	31		

JANUARY

1903: Folklorist and novelist Zora Neale Hurston is born.

monday
7 7

1922: Col. Charles Young, first African American to achieve that rank in the U.S. Army, dies in Lagos, Nigeria.

tuesday
8 8

1866: Fisk Univ. is founded in Nashville, Tenn.
1906: Renowned poet and writer Paul Laurence Dunbar dies.

wednesday
9 9

1864: George Washington Carver, scientist and inventor, is born.

thursday
10 10

1940: Benjamin O. Davis Sr. becomes the U.S. Army's first black general.

friday
11 11

1996: Pioneering sports journalist Sam Skinner dies in Burlingame, Calif.

saturday
12 12

1913: Delta Sigma Theta Sorority, Inc., is founded at Howard University.

sunday
● **13** 13

ANITA PHILYAW

Anita Philyaw graduated from Sarah Lawrence College, where art was one of her majors, and took her M.A. from Columbia University. A native of New York City, Philyaw taught early-childhood classes, designed educational programs for the public school system, and served as an assistant principal. Meanwhile, she has continued to paint and to exhibit her work throughout the New York metropolitan area. Her art, which is held in numerous private collections, always depicts people of color.

Philyaw says of her work: "I want these images to tell you of the strength and power and beauty I see present in the very ordinary activities of life. I take exception to the negative portrayals of people of color that we are inundated with on a daily basis. The whole creative process is an energizing, lifegiving, exciting cycle for me."

Philyaw has been recognized by the Philips Collection (Washington, D.C.). Her art was featured in the *International Review of African-American Art,* published by Hampton University.

AMELIA'S THEME, 1999
Acrylic on canvas, 48 x 28 in.

s	m	t	w	t	f	s
		1	2	3	4	5
6	7	8	9	10	11	12
13	14	15	16	17	18	19
20	21	22	23	24	25	26
27	28	29	30	31		

JANUARY

1940: Julian Bond, civil rights leader and Georgia state senator, is born.

monday
14 14

MARTIN LUTHER KING JR.'S BIRTHDAY
1908: Alpha Kappa Alpha Sorority is founded at Howard Univ. by Ethel Hedgeman Lyle.

tuesday
15 15

1974: Noted singer-composer Leon Bukasa of Zaire dies.

wednesday
16 16

1942: Muhammed Ali, heavyweight boxing champion, is born in Louisville, Ky.

thursday
17 17

1858: Daniel Hale Williams, first physician to perform open-heart surgery and founder of Provident Hospital in Chicago, Ill., is born.

friday
18 18

1918: John H. Johnson, editor and publisher of *Ebony* and *Jet* magazines, is born in Arkansas City, Ark.

saturday
19 19

1893: Bessie Coleman, first female African American aviator, is born in Atlanta, Tex.
2001: Colin Powell sworn in as first African American secretary of state.

sunday
20 20

JANUARY

E. ETHELBERT MILLER

An accomplished author, poet, teacher, and activist, E. Ethelbert Miller is a prominent member of the Washington, D.C., arts community.

Miller, a native of New York City, has served on the faculties of the University of Nevada, Las Vegas, Bennington College, and American University. He was the Jesse Ball DuPont Scholar at Emory and Henry College and scholar-in-residence at George Mason University.

Miller has written six books of poetry and edited three poetry anthologies. His acclaimed anthology *In Search of Color Everywhere* presents more than two hundred poems by African American writers, including Maya Angelou, Alice Walker, Langston Hughes, and Phillis Wheatley. This book won the PEN Oakland Josephine Miles Award in 1994.

Since 1974, Miller has been the director of Howard University's African American Resource Center. He recently published a book of poetry, *Whispers, Secrets and Promises*, and a memoir, *Fathering Words: The Making of an African American Writer*. Miller lives in Washington with his wife and children.

Photograph by Mark Cohen
Courtesy E. Ethelbert Miller

s	m	t	w	t	f	s
		1	2	3	4	5
6	7	8	9	10	11	12
13	14	15	16	17	18	19
20	21	22	23	24	25	26
27	28	29	30	31		

JANUARY

MARTIN LUTHER KING JR. DAY
1993: Congressman Mike Espy of Mississippi is confirmed as Secretary of the Department of Agriculture.

monday ☽ 21 · 21

1906: Pioneering aviator Willa Brown-Chappell is born in Glasgow, Ky.

tuesday 22 · 22

1964: The 24th Amendment is ratified, abolishing the poll tax, which was used as a means of preventing African Americans from voting.

wednesday 23 · 23

1985: Tom Bradley, four-term mayor of Los Angeles, receives the NAACP's Spingarn Medal for public service.

thursday 24 · 24

1966: Constance Baker Motley is the first African American woman to be appointed to a federal judgeship.

friday 25 · 25

1944: Angela Yvonne Davis, political activist and educator, is born in Birmingham, Ala.

saturday 26 · 26

1972: Gospel music legend Mahalia Jackson dies in Evergreen Park, Ill.

sunday 27 · 27

BLACK SEMINOLE INDIAN SCOUTS

Thousands of African slaves fled to the swamps and marshes of Florida. There they formed an alliance with refugees from the Creek and other Indian nations who called themselves Seminole, meaning runaway. From this union emerged the Black Seminole people. As early as the eighteenth century, there were more than 100,000 black Indians.

Assisting the U.S. Army in the Indian wars of the late nineteenth century, the Black Seminole Indian Scouts proved to be skillful fighters and trackers. Shooting with pinpoint accuracy and able to trail three-week-old tracks, the Black Seminoles went through eleven years of battle without a single death or serious wound. But their gallantry failed to win them the land promised under the treaties signed by General Zachary Taylor and President James Polk. Bitterly disillusioned, many of the Scouts left for Mexico, never to return. Today most of the remaining members of the Black Seminole Nation live along the Rio Grande.

Photo courtesy National Archives

s	m	t	w	t	f	s
					1	2
3	4	5	6	7	8	9
10	11	12	13	14	15	16
17	18	19	20	21	22	23
24	25	26	27	28		

FEBRUARY

1944: Matthew Henson receives a joint medal from Congress as codiscoverer of the North Pole.

monday
28 28

1926: Violette Neatley Anderson is the first African American woman admitted to practice before the U.S. Supreme Court.

tuesday
29 29

1844: Richard Theodore Greener is the first African American to graduate from Harvard Univ.

wednesday
30 30

1919: Jackie Robinson, first African American to play in major league baseball, is born.

thursday
31 31

1902: Prolific poet Langston Hughes is born in Joplin, Mo.

friday
1 32

1915: Biologist Ernest E. Just receives the Spingarn Medal for his pioneering research on fertilization and cell division.

saturday
2 33

1948: Portraitist and illustrator Laura Wheeler Waring dies.

sunday
3 34

DR. KENNETH B. CLARKE

Kenneth Clarke (1914–1973) grew up in Harlem, graduated from Howard University, and attended Columbia University, where he became the first African American to receive a Ph.D. in psychology.

In the 1950s, Dr. Clarke's research revealed the effects of school segregation on black children's self-esteem. In his tests, he asked each child, "Which doll is most like you?" while showing them black and white dolls. The responses indicated a negative self-image.

Clarke's research played a pivotal role in the Supreme Court ruling in *Brown v. Board of Education.* He also contributed to Gunnar Myrdal's landmark book on racism, *An American Dilemma.* Clarke's research introduced Americans to the theory that environment is the major influencing factor that shapes a child's behavior. Dr. Clarke held many civic positions in the state of New York and was a member of the State Board of Regents. In 1986, he founded a firm to provide consultation on racial issues.

Photograph by John W. Mosley

Courtesy Charles L. Blockson, African American Collection, Temple University

s	m	t	w	t	f	s
					1	2
3	4	5	6	7	8	9
10	11	12	13	14	15	16
17	18	19	20	21	22	23
24	25	26	27	28		

FEBRUARY

1913: Rosa Parks, initiator of the Montgomery, Ala., bus boycott, is born.

monday

(**4** 35

1934: Hank Aaron, major league baseball home run king, is born.

tuesday

5 36

1993: Arthur Ashe, tennis player, humanitarian, and activist, dies.

wednesday

6 37

1926: Negro History Week, originated by Carter G. Woodson, is observed for the first time.

thursday

7 38

1990: CBS-TV suspends Andy Rooney from *60 Minutes* for three months for making purportedly antigay and antiblack remarks in a magazine interview.

friday

8 39

1944: Alice Walker, Pulitzer Prize–winning author, is born.

saturday

9 40

1927: Leontyne Price, internationally acclaimed opera singer, is born in Laurel, Miss.

sunday

10 41

FEBRUARY

MARDI GRAS INDIANS

The Mardi Gras Indian tradition emerged as a celebration practiced exclusively by African Americans who drew on Amerindian, African, and West Indian rhythms and motifs to create a folk ritual unique to New Orleans.

Since the early history of New Orleans, cultural distinctions (French, Spanish, and Anglo) have caused antagonism between the uptown and downtown districts. This rivalry was adopted by the African Americans and subsequently exhibited by "Indian tribes" from the respective neighborhoods. Early tribes fought with guns, knives, and hatchets. In recent decades, the physical conflict has transformed into aesthetic competition.

Photographer J. Nash Porter's career combines documentary and commercial photography with photojournalism. A New Orleans native, Porter is best known for his work with the Mardi Gras Indians. He remarks, "Through the lens of my camera, I share with others the exciting tradition that I grew up with. Hopefully I can ignite a spark of enthusiasm and bring about an awareness in other communities of the New Orleans Mardi Gras Indians."
—Dr. Joyce M. Jackson

Photograph courtesy J. Nash Porter, photographer

s	m	t	w	t	f	s
					1	2
3	4	5	6	7	8	9
10	11	12	13	14	15	16
17	18	19	20	21	22	23
24	25	26	27	28		

FEBRUARY

1990: Nelson Mandela is released from a South African prison after being detained for 27 years as a political prisoner.

monday
11 42

LINCOLN'S BIRTHDAY
1896: Isaac Burns Murphy, greatest jockey of all time, dies.

tuesday
● **12** 43

ASH WEDNESDAY
1970: Joseph L. Searles becomes the first black member of the New York Stock Exchange.

wednesday
13 44

VALENTINE'S DAY
1817: Frederick Douglass, "the Great Emancipator," is born.

thursday
14 45

1961: U.S. protestors and African nationalists disrupt UN sessions to protest the slaying of Congo premier Patrice Lumumba.

friday
15 46

1923: Bessie Smith makes her first recording, "Down Hearted Blues," which sells 800,000 copies for Columbia Records.

saturday
16 47

1938: Mary Frances Berry, first woman to serve as chancellor of a major research university (Univ. of Colorado), is born in Nashville, Tenn.

sunday
17 48

HULAN JACK

Born in British Guyana, Hulan Jack (1906–1987) came to the United States at the age of sixteen. He is most noted for being the first black borough president in New York City. In 1944 Adam Clayton Powell was elected to the U.S. Congress; this historic achievement set the stage for other blacks—like Constance Baker Motley, Percy Sutton, David Dinkins, and Hulan Jack—who later assumed high political office in the state of New York. Jack served as Harlem representative in the New York State Assembly from 1940 to 1952; he was elected to the borough presidency of Manhattan in 1953.

Throughout his career, Jack played an influential role in the Democratic Party of New York State. In 1956, Borough President Hulan Jack tried to entice the New York Giants baseball team to remain in New York by promising a new 110,000-seat stadium. But the Giants management ultimately refused his offer and eventually moved the team to California.

Photo courtesy National Archives

s	m	t	w	t	f	s
					1	2
3	4	5	6	7	8	9
10	11	12	13	14	15	16
17	18	19	20	21	22	23
24	25	26	27	28		

FEBRUARY

PRESIDENTS' DAY

monday
18 49

1688: Quakers at Germantown, Pa., adopt the first formal antislavery resolution in American history.

1919: The First Pan-African Congress is held in Paris, France.

tuesday
19 50

1927: Sidney Poitier, first African American to win an Academy Award in a starring role, is born in Miami, Fla.

wednesday
☽ 20 51

1965: El-Hajj Malik El-Shabazz (Malcolm X), American black nationalist, is assassinated.

thursday
21 52

WASHINGTON'S BIRTHDAY

friday
22 53

1841: Grafton Tyler Brown, one of California's first African American painters, is born.

1972: Political activist Angela Davis is released from jail.

saturday
23 54

1966: Military leaders oust Kwame Nkrumah, president of Ghana, while he is in Peking on a peace mission to stop the Vietnam War.

sunday
24 55

FEB/MAR

JEANNE ROREX

Jeanne Rorex became interested in traditional Indian art forms through the carvings of her uncle, Cherokee sculptor Willard Stone. She studied at Bacone College under master Cheyenne artist Dick West. Combining this training with her rural Eastern Oklahoma roots and her interpretation of her Cherokee ancestors' heritage, Rorex's work has become nationally recognized and appreciated.

Rorex's painting is strong in subject and feeling, yet simple and calm. Of *At Day's End*, she observes: "In the Indian Territories [eastern Oklahoma], most families were mixed blood and most were farmers. Neighbors often shared the work in the fields. . . . These two young women are enjoying a quiet visit under the early moon, at the end of a long day."

Rorex's work has won numerous awards and many solo exhibitions. "My painting opens a door to better understanding of individual feelings and experiences . . . of human relationships and emotions. I am a lucky woman!"

AT DAY'S END, 1991

Acrylic on canvas, 18 x 12 in.

s	m	t	w	t	f	s
					1	2
3	4	5	6	7	8	9
10	11	12	13	14	15	16
17	18	19	20	21	22	23
24	25	26	27	28	29	30
31					MARCH	

PURIM (BEGINS AT SUNSET)

1978: Daniel "Chappie" James, first African American four-star general, dies in Colorado Springs, Colo.

monday
25 56

1928: Singer Antoine "Fats" Domino is born.

tuesday
26 57

1902: Marian Anderson, world-renowned opera singer and civil rights advocate, is born in Philadelphia, Pa.

wednesday
○ **27** 58

1948: Sgt. Cornelius F. Adjetey becomes the first martyr for national independence of Ghana.

thursday
28 59

1914: Ralph Waldo Ellison, author of the award-winning *Invisible Man*, is born in Oklahoma City, Okla.

friday
1 60

1955: Claudette Colvin refuses to give up her seat on a bus in Montgomery, Ala., nine months before Rosa Parks's arrest for the same action sparks the Montgomery bus boycott.

saturday
2 61

1821: Thomas L. Jennings is the first African American to be granted a patent in the United States, for his technique to "dry-scour" clothes.

sunday
3 62

MARCH

BOB HAYES

As a student at Florida A&M, "Bullet" Bob Hayes won the national collegiate title for the 200-yard dash and secured the Amateur Athletic Union 100-yard-dash title three times. Hayes later became the first to run the 100-yard dash in 9.1 seconds. In the 1964 Olympics, he won two golds—in the 100 meters, and as anchor to the record-setting 4 x 100-yard relay team.

Hayes was drafted by the Dallas Cowboys in 1964. His success as a wide receiver helped make the Cowboys a winning franchise. He was the first Cowboy to have 1,000 yards receiving, had the highest yard average per catch, the longest reception (a 95-yard touchdown), the longest punt return (90 yards for a touchdown), and the most touchdowns scored by a receiver (71).

Hayes's exceptional speed and power on the field catalyzed a major change in professional football: opposing coaches developed the zone defense because no defensive back could cover Hayes man to man.

Hayes now lives in Jacksonville, Florida, where the Bob Hayes Track & Field Invitational Meet is held annually in his honor.

Photograph courtesy National Archives

s	m	t	w	t	f	s
					1	2
3	4	5	6	7	8	9
10	11	12	13	14	15	16
17	18	19	20	21	22	23
24	25	26	27	28	29	30
31						MARCH

1932: Zensi Miriam Makeba, "Empress of African Song," is born.

monday
4 63

1770: Crispus Attucks is killed in the Boston Massacre, marking the start of the American Revolution.

tuesday
5 64

1857: U.S. Supreme Court rules against citizenship for African Americans in the Dred Scott decision.

wednesday
☾ **6** 65

1539: Estevanico or Esteban de Dorantes, native of Azamoor, Morocco, sets out to explore what is now the southwestern United States.

thursday
7 66

1876: After three years of controversy, U.S. Senate refuses to seat P. B. S. Pinchback, elected as Louisiana senator in 1873.

friday
8 67

1919: Nora Douglas Holt and other black Chicago musicians form the Chicago Musical Association.

saturday
9 68

MOTHERING SUNDAY (U.K.)

1845: Women's rights activist Hallie Quinn Brown is born in Pittsburgh, Pa.

sunday
10 69

MARCH

MAHALIA JACKSON

Mahalia Jackson, "the Queen of Gospel Song," was born in New Orleans. Her father was a preacher at a small church. Jackson (1911–1972) wasn't allowed to listen to jazz or blues at home, but she listened to the blues of Bessie Smith and operatic music at a friend's house. Though she loved the blues, her musical interests centered on singing spirituals in her father's choir.

She left school in the eighth grade to join a traveling quintet. In her years on the road, she saved her money to open a beauty salon and flower shop. But she also kept singing.

In 1945, Jackson received international acclaim for her recording "Move on Up a Little Higher." Her fame spread rapidly, and her first Carnegie Hall concert, in 1950, was a sold-out performance.

As a New York music critic aptly predicted, Jackson "will always be noted for her vibrant, expressive contralto voice and her intensely moving interpretations of gospel songs."

Photograph courtesy National Archives

1948: Dr. Reginald Weir of New York City wins his first match in the USLTA Championship Tournament.

monday

11 70

1791: Benjamin Banneker and Pierre Charles L'Enfant are commissioned to plan and develop Washington, D.C.

tuesday

12 71

1773: Jean Baptist Pointe du Sable founds the city of Chicago.

wednesday

13 72

1933: Composer, musician, and producer Quincy Delight Jones is born.

thursday

● **14** 73

1947: John Lee becomes the first African American commissioned officer in the U.S. Navy.

friday

15 74

1827: John Russwurm, first African American college graduate, begins publication of Freedom's *Journal* with Samuel Cornish.

saturday

16 75

---

s	m	t	w	t	f	s
					1	2
3	4	5	6	7	8	9
10	11	12	13	14	15	16
17	18	19	20	21	22	23
24	25	26	27	28	29	30
31					MARCH	

ST. PATRICK'S DAY

1867: Educator Ida Rebecca Cummings is born in Baltimore, Md.

sunday

17 76

HOWARD THURMAN

Howard Thurman (1899–1981) touched many lives through his lectures, sermons, books, and consultations. A host of notable leaders subscribed to the spiritual doctrines he preached.

Thurman grew up in segregated Daytona Beach, Florida, and was the first black person in the state to finish the eighth grade. He studied the religious thought of diverse cultures and later integrated those philosophies into his own teachings. In 1935 he led a delegation to India, where he spoke with Mahatma Mohandas Gandhi. The encounter further inspired his vision of world peace and unification.

In 1953, Boston University named Thurman Dean of Marsh Chapel, a position never before held by an African-American.

Thurman and his wife, Sue Bailey Thurman, met with Dr. Martin Luther King Jr. on many occasions. The Thurmans introduced Dr. King to Gandhi's principles of nonviolent resistance.

The Howard Thurman memorial, on the campus of Morehouse College in Atlanta, Georgia, honors a great religious leader.

Photograph courtesy National Archives

s	m	t	w	t	f	s
					1	2
3	4	5	6	7	8	9
10	11	12	13	14	15	16
17	18	19	20	21	22	23
24	25	26	27	28	29	30
31					MARCH	

BANK HOLIDAY (N. IRELAND)

1901: William H. Johnson, premier painter, is born in Florence, S.C.

monday
18 77

1930: Jazz saxophonist Ornette Coleman is born in Fort Worth, Tex.

tuesday
19 78

VERNAL EQUINOX 7:16 P.M. (GMT)

1883: Jan Matzeliger receives a patent for the shoe-lasting machine, which launches mass production of shoes.

wednesday
20 79

1965: Martin Luther King Jr. leads thousands of marchers from Selma to Montgomery, Ala., to dramatize denial of voting rights to African Americans.

thursday
21 80

1492: Alonzo Pietro, explorer, sets sail with Christopher Columbus.

friday
☽ **22** 81

1985: Patricia Roberts Harris, former Cabinet member and ambassador, dies.

saturday
23 82

PALM SUNDAY

1907: Nurse and aviator Janet Harmon Bragg is born in Griffin, Ga.

sunday
24 83

MARCH

BLANCHE CALLOWAY

Blanche Calloway (1902–1978) was born in Baltimore, Maryland. Her father was a lawyer; her mother was a schoolteacher and a strong musical influence on Blanche and her brother Cab.

Calloway began singing in church. She left college to pursue a career in show business, performing in traveling musicals, and sang on Broadway in the famous African American musical *Shuffle Along.* When she landed a role in the Chicago production of *Plantation Days,* she took Cab along, intending to help him through law school. But Cab, too, was set on a musical career; he would soon be famous for his "hi-de-ho."

In 1930, Calloway became the first woman to form and lead an all-male band. She performed with the band for eleven years, traveling throughout the United States. Around 1953, Calloway moved to Florida; there she started a mail-order cosmetics business called Afram House—the first of its kind to be owned and operated by an African American.

Photograph courtesy Charles L. Blockson, African American Collection, Temple University

s	m	t	w	t	f	s
					1	2
3	4	5	6	7	8	9
10	11	12	13	14	15	16
17	18	19	20	21	22	23
24	25	26	27	28	29	30
31					MARCH	

1931: Ida B. Wells-Barnett, journalist, antilynching activist, and founding member of the NAACP, dies in Chicago, Ill.

monday
25 84

1886: Hugh N. Mulzac, the first black American to be captain of an American merchant marine ship (SS *Booker T. Washington,* 1942), is born in the West Indies.

tuesday
26 85

FIRST NIGHT OF PASSOVER

1924: Jazz singer Sarah Vaughan, "the Divine One," is born in Newark, N.J.

wednesday
27 86

SECOND NIGHT OF PASSOVER

1870: Jonathan S. Wright becomes the first African American state supreme court justice in South Carolina.

thursday
28 87

GOOD FRIDAY

1918: Singer and actor Pearl Bailey is born in Newport News, Va.

friday
29 88

1963: Capt. Edward J. Dwight Jr. becomes a candidate for astronaut training.

saturday
30 89

EASTER SUNDAY
SUMMER TIME BEGINS (U.K.)

1871: Jack Johnson, first African American heavyweight boxing champion, is born.

sunday
31 90

APRIL

JUDGE WILLIAM H. HASTIE JR.

William H. Hastie Jr. (1904–1976) was born in Knoxville, Tennessee. When his father took a job in Washington, D.C., young William enrolled in Dunbar High School; he excelled on the track team and was valedictorian of his class. He attended college at Amherst in Massachusetts, and went on to graduate from Harvard Law School, fourteenth in his class.

In 1946, Hastie was appointed the first black governor of the Virgin Islands by President Harry Truman. Three years later he became the first black federal appeals judge in the United States. Hastie worked to end racial discrimination on all fronts, particularly in the military. Though he made significant progress, he became frustrated by the armed forces' continuing seg-regation policies, and resigned.

Hastie was nominated again by President Truman to a judgeship on the U.S. Court of Appeals for the Third Circuit. Senate confirmation was slow, thanks to Hastie's involvement with the NAACP, but he was confirmed in 1950 and served the court until 1971.

Photograph courtesy National Archives

s	m	t	w	t	f	s
	1	2	3	4	5	6
7	8	9	10	11	12	13
14	15	16	17	18	19	20
21	22	23	24	25	26	27
28	29	30				

APRIL

EASTER MONDAY (CANADA, U.K.)

1930: Zawditu, first female monarch of Ethiopia, dies.

monday

1 91

1796: Haitian revolt leader Toussaint L'Ouverture commands French forces at Santo Domingo.

tuesday

2 92

1984: John Thompson of Georgetown Univ. is the first African American coach to win an NCAA basketball tournament.

wednesday

3 93

1968: Martin Luther King Jr. is assassinated in Memphis, Tenn.

thursday

☾ 4 94

1937: Colin Powell, first African American to serve as chief of staff of the armed forces and secretary of state, is born in New York, N.Y.

friday

5 95

1905: W. Warrick Cardozo, physician and pioneering researcher into sickle cell anemia, is born in Washington, D.C.

saturday

6 96

DAYLIGHT SAVING TIME BEGINS

1915: Jazz and blues legend Billie Holiday is born in East Baltimore, Md.

sunday

7 97

APRIL

JAMES BECKWOURTH

James Beckwourth (1798–1864) was a contemporary of Kit Carson, Davy Crockett, and Daniel Boone—and, like them, he was tough enough to succeed in the Wild West. Beckwourth was an expert trapper and marksman. Born a slave, he lived among Native American tribes from 1826 to 1834, including the Absaroka (Crow) people. From them he earned various names acknowledging his honor and bravery—first White Handled Knife, then Morning Star (in 1856, when he was made a tribal leader), and, later, Antelope.

In 1844, Beckwourth discovered a passage through the Sierra Nevada while leading a wagon train of settlers. Now called Beckwourth Pass, it became an overland wagon route to the upper Sacramento Valley. Beckwourth carried the mail by horseback from Monterey to southern California in 1847. It is believed that he was poisoned by the Absaroka people during a visit in 1864, to keep him from returning to live among people in the outside world.

Photograph courtesy African American Museum and Library at Oakland

s	m	t	w	t	f	s
	1	2	3	4	5	6
7	8	9	10	11	12	13
14	15	16	17	18	19	20
21	22	23	24	25	26	27
28	29	30				

APRIL

1974: Hank Aaron breaks Babe Ruth's major league record with 715 home runs.

monday
8 98

1898: Actor and singer Paul Robeson is born in Princeton, N.J.

tuesday
9 99

1943: Arthur Ashe, first African American to win the U.S. Open and men's singles title at Wimbledon, is born in Richmond, Va.

wednesday
10 100

1996: Forty-three African nations sign the African Nuclear Weapons Free Zone Treaty, pledging not to build, bury, stockpile, or test nuclear weapons.

thursday
11 101

1966: Emmett Ashford becomes the first African American major league umpire.

friday
● **12** 102

1907: Harlem Hospital opens in New York City.

saturday
13 103

1775: First U.S. abolitionist society is founded in Pennsylvania; Ben Franklin is its president.

sunday
14 104

HAZEL SCOTT

Determination, talent, impatience with racial segregation, and supreme confidence were the defining traits of Hazel Scott (1920–1981)—jazz singer, actor, and political activist. Born in Trinidad, Scott mastered the piano and other instruments at an early age. In 1924 the family moved to the United States, where Scott's talents won her a scholarship to the Juilliard School of Music. Her critically acclaimed debut at New York's Town Hall, and her trumpet and piano performance in her mother's All Woman Orchestra, paved the way for her role as saxophonist with Louis Armstrong's All Girl Band.

In 1945, Scott married Congressman Adam Clayton Powell Jr., a firebrand preacher and civil rights revolutionary. Acutely aware of the injustice facing African American entertainers, Scott refused to perform for segregated audiences. Her premier nightclub acts, noteworthy Broadway shows, and successful films led in 1950 to the first nationally syndicated musical variety television program hosted by an African American woman, *The Hazel Scott Show.*

Photograph courtesy National Archives

s	m	t	w	t	f	s
	1	2	3	4	5	6
7	8	9	10	11	12	13
14	15	16	17	18	19	20
21	22	23	24	25	26	27
28	29	30				

APRIL

1889: Asa Phillip Randolph, labor leader and civil rights advocate, is born in Crescent Way, Fla.

monday
15 105

1864: Acclaimed soprano-baritone singer Flora Batson is born in Washington, D.C.

tuesday
16 106

1758: Frances Williams, first African American to graduate from college in the Western Hemisphere, publishes a collection of Latin poems.

wednesday
17 107

1818: A regiment of Indians and blacks is defeated in the Battle of Suwanna, Fla., ending the first Seminole War.

thursday
18 108

1938: Nana Annor Adjaye, Pan-Africanist, dies in West Nzima, Ghana.

friday
19 109

1909: Jazz musician Lionel Hampton is born in Louisville, Ky.
1984: Popular English vocalist Mabel Mercer dies.

saturday
☽ **20** 110

1966: Pfc. Milton Lee Olive is awarded the Medal of Honor posthumously for bravery during the Vietnam War.

sunday
21 111

MERVYN DYMALLY

Born in Cedros, Trinidad, in 1926, Mervyn Dymally immigrated to the United States in 1946 to study at Lincoln University in Jefferson City, Missouri. He earned a B.A. degree in education from California State University in 1954 and began teaching school in Los Angeles. Subsequently, he began a political career and became the first black elected to the California senate, the only black to serve as lieutenant governor of the state (1975), and the first foreign-born black to serve in Congress (1980). Dymally defeated four other candidates to win the primary in California's Thirty-First Congressional District. From 1987 to 1989, he was chairman of the Congressional Black Caucus. Today, Dymally heads an international consulting firm in Los Angeles.

Photograph courtesy the African American Museum and Library at Oakland

---

EARTH DAY

1922: Bassist, composer, and bandleader Charles Mingus is born.

monday

22 112

1856: Granville T. Woods, inventor of the steam boiler and automobile air brakes, is born.

tuesday

23 113

1993: Oliver Tambo, leader of the African National Congress, dies in Johannesburg, South Africa.

wednesday

24 114

1918: Ella Fitzgerald, "First Lady of Song," is born in Newport News, Va.

thursday

25 115

1991: Maryann Bishop Coffey becomes the first female African American cochair of the National Conference of Christians and Jews.

friday

26 116

1994: South Africa's first all-races democratic elections are held.

saturday

○ **27** 117

1913: Political activist Margaret Just Butcher is born in Washington, D.C.

sunday

28 118

s	m	t	w	t	f	s
	1	2	3	4	5	6
7	8	9	10	11	12	13
14	15	16	17	18	19	20
21	22	23	24	25	26	27
28	29	30				

APRIL

HENRY FLIPPER

Henry Flipper (1877–1940) was the first black to graduate from West Point, in 1877, and the first black to be assigned to a command position in a black unit after the Civil War. However, Flipper became the victim of a controversial court-martial proceeding—he was charged with "conduct unbecoming an officer and a gentleman"—and received a dishonorable discharge. Flipper made repeated attempts to vindicate himself, but at the time of his death, he still had not cleared his record. Years later, however, the sentence was reversed. He was posthumously given an honorable discharge, and his remains were reburied in Arlington Cemetery with full honors.

As a citizen, Flipper worked as a special agent for the Department of Justice, where his fluency in Spanish aided in saving thousands of acres of disputed land in the Southwest. His published translations of Spanish and Mexican laws continue to be standard reference material today.

Photograph courtesy National Archives

s	m	t	w	t	f	s
			1	2	3	4
5	6	7	8	9	10	11
12	13	14	15	16	17	18
19	20	21	22	23	24	25
26	27	28	29	30	31	

MAY

1992: Four Los Angeles police officers are acquitted of charges stemming from the beating of Rodney King; rioting ensues.

monday

29 119

1951: Surgeons Rivers Frederick, Ulysses G. Dailey, and Nelson M. Russell are honored at the Univ. of Italy.

tuesday

30 120

1950: Gwendolyn Brooks becomes the first African American to win the Pulitzer Prize, for her book of poetry *Annie Allen.*

wednesday

1 121

1969: Record-breaking cricket batsman Brian Lara is born in Santa Cruz, Trinidad.

thursday

2 122

1855: Macon B. Allen is the first African American to be formally admitted to the bar in Massachusetts.

friday

3 123

1969: *No Place to Be Somebody* opens in New York. It will win the Pulitzer Prize the following year.

saturday

☾ **4** 124

CINCO DE MAYO

sunday

1905: Robert Sengstacke Abbott founds the *Chicago Defender* with a capital outlay of twenty-five cents.

5 125

LIONEL HAMPTON

Lionel Hampton is one of the last surviving links to the beginnings of jazz music. The young "Hamp," already established as a drummer, got his break in 1930: he was hired to accompany Louis Armstrong during a recording session at NBC's Hollywood studio. Armstrong noticed a vibraphone sitting in the corner (it had been used to record NBC's familiar three-tone station identification). He asked Hamp—who had never played a vibraphone before—to play the instrument on his recording. The song they recorded during that session, "Memories of You," is a classic standard.

In Hampton's next major move, he joined the Benny Goodman quintet. This band, according to musicologist Frank Tirro, "established Hampton as one of the best musicians of the era, a master of swing, and a performer of technical virtuosity." Hampton performed at the inaugural celebrations of six presidents, beginning with Harry Truman. He continues to entertain audiences worldwide, maintaining a hectic touring schedule.

Photograph by John W. Mosley

Photograph courtesy Charles L. Blockson, African American Collection, Temple University

s	m	t	w	t	f	s
			1	2	3	4
5	6	7	8	9	10	11
12	13	14	15	16	17	18
19	20	21	22	23	24	25
26	27	28	29	30	31	

MAY

BANK HOLIDAY (U.K.)

1995: Ron Kirk becomes the first black mayor of Dallas, Tex., with 62 percent of the vote.

monday

6 126

1946: William H. Hastie is inaugurated as the first black governor of the Virgin Islands.

tuesday

7 127

1958: Ernest Green is the first black to graduate from Central High School in Little Rock, Ark.

wednesday

8 128

1800: John Brown, abolitionist and martyr at Harpers Ferry, is born.

thursday

9 129

1968: A public school in Brooklyn, N.Y., is named for noted scientist and inventor Lewis H. Latimer.

friday

10 130

1895: William Grant Still, dean of black classical composers, is born.

saturday

11 131

MOTHER'S DAY

1926: Mervyn Dymally, California's first African American lieutenant governor, is born in Cedros, Trinidad.

sunday

● **12** 132

MAY

ALTHEA GIBSON

Althea Gibson (b. 1927) was one of the world's greatest tennis players. She dominated women's tennis in 1957 and 1958, years in which she won consecutive Wimbledon and U.S. Open titles.

In her teens, Gibson showed tremendous potential when trading shots with a pro at the Cosmopolitan Tennis Club in New York. The members were so impressed that they bought her a junior membership, setting in motion a series of events that would change tennis forever.

By 1950 the racial barriers in tennis had crumbled, and Althea heroically battled the Wimbledon champion, Louise Brough, before succumbing 9–7 in the third set of the Nationals at Forest Hills. She lost the match but gained confidence; in 1957 she won her first Wimbledon championship, defeating her doubles partner Darlene Hard (shown here) in straight sets.

In 2000, Venus Williams became the first African American woman to win Wimbledon since Althea Gibson's history-making victory in 1957. Williams remarked that Gibson had wished her luck and was watching the game.

Photograph courtesy National Archives

s	m	t	w	t	f	s
			1	2	3	4
5	6	7	8	9	10	11
12	13	14	15	16	17	18
19	20	21	22	23	24	25
26	27	28	29	30	31	

MAY

1914: Heavyweight boxer Joe Louis, "the Brown Bomber," is born in Lexington, Ala.

monday
13 133

1913: Clara Stanton Jones, first African American president of the American Library Association, is born in St. Louis, Mo.

tuesday
14 134

1918: Pfc. Henry Johnson and Pfc. Needham Roberts receive the Croix de Guerre for their service in World War I, becoming the first Americans to win France's highest military award.

wednesday
15 135

1929: John Conyers Jr., founder of the Congressional Black Caucus, is born.

thursday
16 136

1954: The U.S. Supreme Court declares school segregation unconstitutional in *Brown v. Board of Education*.

friday
17 137

ARMED FORCES DAY

1955: Mary McLeod Bethune, educator and founder of the National Council of Negro Women, dies in Daytona Beach, Fla.

saturday
18 138

1993: Univ. of Virginia professor Rita Dove is appointed U.S. Poet Laureate.

sunday
☽ **19** 139

BISHOP C. M. "DADDY" GRACE

There is a long history of evangelists espousing spiritual doctrines that differ from those of the traditional Christian churches. Some have won substantial followings and substantial wealth. Bishop "Daddy" Grace (1881–1960) was one of the most successful.

Grace was born in the Cape Verde Islands off west Africa. In 1903 his family immigrated to New Bedford, Massachusetts, where he took on odd jobs before founding his first church around 1923. His United House of Prayer for All People became one of the largest and wealthiest U.S. churches. It still exists today, in more than one hundred U.S. cities and in England, Egypt, Cape Verde, and Portugal. At the time of his death, Grace's personal worth was about $6 million.

On January 12, 1960, "Daddy" Grace died of a heart attack. These words are engraved on his New Bedford tombstone: "Peace I Bring, Peace I Give, Peace I Leave," and "BYE FOR NOW" in very large letters.

Photograph by John W. Mosley

Photograph courtesy Charles L. Blockson, African American Collection, Temple University

s	m	t	w	t	f	s
			1	2	3	4
5	6	7	8	9	10	11
12	13	14	15	16	17	18
19	20	21	22	23	24	25
26	27	28	29	30	31	

MAY

VICTORIA DAY (CANADA)

1868: P. B. S. Pinchback and James J. Harris are the first African American delegates to the Republican National Convention.

monday
20 140

1833: African American students enroll in classes at Oberlin College, Oberlin, Ohio.

tuesday
21 141

1967: Noted poet Langston Hughes dies in New York City.

wednesday
22 142

1832: Jamaican national figure Samuel Sharpe is hanged.

thursday
23 143

1905: Distinguished educator Hilda Davis is born in Washington, D.C.

friday
24 144

1963: African Liberation Day is declared at the conference of the Organization of African Unity in Addis Ababa, Ethiopia.

saturday
25 145

1926: Renowned jazz trumpeter Miles Davis is born in Alton, Ill.

sunday
○ **26** 146

DR. ANDREW FOSTER

A pioneer in education for the deaf, Dr. Andrew J. Foster (1925–1987) was instrumental in founding twenty-two schools and an equal number of religious programs for deaf children in more than twenty African countries.

Born in Birmingham, Alabama, Foster lost his hearing at eleven after contracting spinal meningitis. Drawn to a career in education, he attended the Alabama School for the Negro Deaf in Talladega and, in 1954, became the first African American to graduate from Gallaudet College in Washington, D.C. After obtaining his master's degree, Foster set out to achieve his childhood dream of establishing schools for deaf students.

In 1956, Foster founded the Christian Mission for Deaf Africans, and a year later he opened the Accra Mission School for the Deaf in Accra, Ghana. He also established a boarding school for deaf children in Mampong-Akwapim, near Accra, and a mission in Ibadan, Nigeria. The establishment of these institutions marked the beginning of education for the deaf in Africa.

Photograph courtesy Gallaudet University Archives

s	m	t	w	t	f	s
						1
2	3	4	5	6	7	8
9	10	11	12	13	14	15
16	17	18	19	20	21	22
23	24	25	26	27	28	29
30						JUNE

MEMORIAL DAY OBSERVED
BANK HOLIDAY (U.K.)

monday
27 147

1942: Dorie Miller, a messman, is awarded the Navy Cross for heroism at Pearl Harbor.

1981: Jazz pianist Mary Lou Williams dies in Durham, N.C.

tuesday
28 148

1973: Tom Bradley becomes the first African American mayor of Los Angeles.

wednesday
29 149

MEMORIAL DAY

thursday
30 150

1965: Vivian Malone is the first black to graduate from the Univ. of Alabama.

1955: The U.S. Supreme Court orders school integration "with all deliberate speed."

friday
31 151

1919: Noted physician Caroline Virginia Still Wiley Anderson dies in Philadelphia, Pa.

saturday
1 152

1948: Jamaican-born track star Herb McKenley sets a new world record for the 400-yard dash.

sunday
2 153

JUNE

WOMEN'S ARMY CORPS—
6888TH POSTAL DIRECTORY
BATTALION

The Women's Army Corps (WAC) was established during World War II "for the purpose of making available to the national defense the knowledge, skill, and special training of the women of the nation." It sprang from the WAAC, whose members did not receive the full benefits granted to male soldiers. Though there was strong resistance to women in the army, Oveta Culp Hobby, the unit's commander, promoted the idea that each woman serving would release a man for combat. As clerical workers, radio operators, electricians, and air traffic controllers, more than 150,000 women performed important duties overseas and at home.

On May 27, 1945, these black women members of the 6888th Postal Directory Battalion paraded in honor of the French heroine, Joan of Arc. The parade took place at the Place du Vieux Marche in Rouen, where Joan d'Arc was burned at the stake in 1431 for heresy and witchcraft. (She was exonerated and canonized in 1920.)

Photograph courtesy National Archives

1904: Charles R. Drew, originator of blood plasma banks, is born in Washington, D.C.

monday

☾ **3** 154

1967: Bill Cosby receives an Emmy Award for his work in the television series *I Spy.*

tuesday

4 155

1973: Doris A. Davis of Compton, Calif., becomes the first African American woman to govern a city in a major metropolitan area.

wednesday

5 156

1939: Marian Wright Edelman, first African American woman to be admitted to the Mississippi bar and founder of the Children's Defense Fund, is born.

thursday

6 157

1994: The Organization of African Unity formally admits South Africa as its fifty-third member.

friday

7 158

1939: Herb Adderley, Hall of Famer and defensive back for the Green Bay Packers, is born in Philadelphia, Pa.

saturday

8 159

---

s	m	t	w	t	f	s
						1
2	3	4	5	6	7	8
9	10	11	12	13	14	15
16	17	18	19	20	21	22
23	24	25	26	27	28	29
30					JUNE	

1877: Renowned sculptor Meta Vaux Warrick is born in Philadelphia, Pa.

sunday

9 160

SCOTTSBORO BOYS TRIAL

The case of the Scottsboro Boys is one of the best-known trials in history. On March 25, 1931, nine African American males, ages thirteen to twenty-one, were jailed and accused of gang-raping two white women on a freight train.

Haywood Patterson (pictured) and the other Boys were on that train. Also on the train were four young whites, two males and two females. A stone-throwing fight broke out when one of the white males stepped on Patterson's hand while he was hanging onto the side of the train. When the melee was over, all but one of the whites had been forced off the train and a posse was waiting at the next stop—Paint Rock, Alabama—to arrest the black youths.

The charges against four of the Boys were dismissed; the others served long prison terms. Law historian Douglas O. Linder wrote, "No crime in American history— let alone a crime that never occurred—produced as many trials, convictions, reversals, and retrials."

Photograph courtesy National Archives

s	m	t	w	t	f	s
						1
2	3	4	5	6	7	8
9	10	11	12	13	14	15
16	17	18	19	20	21	22
23	24	25	26	27	28	29
30						JUNE

1854: James Augustine Healy, first African American Catholic bishop in the United States, is ordained a priest in Notre Dame Cathedral.

monday
10 161

1964: Nelson Mandela is sentenced to life imprisonment by the South African government.

tuesday
11 162

1963: Civil rights leader Medgar Evers is killed in Jackson, Miss.

wednesday
12 163

1967: Thurgood Marshall is appointed to the U.S. Supreme Court by President Lyndon B. Johnson.

thursday
13 164

FLAG DAY

friday
14 165

1989: Congressman William Gray is elected Democratic whip of the House of Representatives, the highest leadership position in Congress held thus far by an African American.

1927: Natalie Hinderas, a musical prodigy who will give her first recital at age eight, is born in Oberlin, Ohio.

saturday
15 166

FATHER'S DAY

sunday
16 167

1976: Students riot in Soweto, South Africa.

JUNE

JANET COLLINS

Janet Collins was born in 1923 in New Orleans. Her family moved to Los Angeles, and she attended Los Angeles City College and studied art at the Los Angeles Art Center School. A talented painter, Collins sold her artworks to help finance a move to New York City, where she pursued a career in dance.

Collins's talent got her a position with the Katherine Dunham Troupe. But the Ballets Russes de Monte Carlo rejected her because of her color, then offered her a position if she would paint her skin white; she refused.

In 1949, Janet Collins made her New York debut in a solo show. For the next couple of years, she was the lead dancer in Cole Porter's musical *Out of This World,* for which she received the Donaldson Award. In 1951 she joined the Metropolitan Opera and the following year became the first black prima ballerina. Collins has taught at several colleges since she retired from dancing; she now lives in Seattle.

Photograph courtesy Library of Congress

s	m	t	w	t	f	s
						1
2	3	4	5	6	7	8
9	10	11	12	13	14	15
16	17	18	19	20	21	22
23	24	25	26	27	28	29
30					JUNE	

1871: James Weldon Johnson, writer, poet, and first African American to be admitted to the Florida bar, is born.

monday

17 168

1942: The U.S. Navy commissions its first black officer, Harvard Univ. medical student Bernard Whitfield Robinson.

tuesday

☽ **18** 169

JUNETEENTH

1862: News of the Emancipation Proclamation reaches the South and Texas through Gen. Gordon Granger.

wednesday

19 170

1858: Charles Waddell Chesnutt, first African American writer in the United States to receive critical literary acclaim, is born.

thursday

20 171

SUMMER SOLSTICE 1:24 P.M. (GMT)

1859: Renowned painter Henry Ossawa Tanner is born.

friday

21 172

1909: Katherine Dunham, revolutionary force in modern dance, is born in Joliet, Ill.

saturday

22 173

1899: Pvt. George Wanton is cited for bravery at Tayabacoa, Cuba, in the Spanish-American War.

sunday

23 174

YVONNE BROWNE

Yvonne Browne was born in Queens, New York, of West Indian parents. The island culture tends to dominate her art, showing clearly in her use of bright colors and warm figures, and also in her outlook. "I could never do negative art. I try to have something beautiful in everything I do."

As a child, Yvonne drew and painted constantly, on everything in sight. "My mother was forever cleaning the walls," she remembers. Eventually she attended an arts-and-music high school and, later, Queens College, where she received a degree in fine arts. Browne first achieved recognition for her batik images. But because the process was so exhausting, she stopped working in batik and started doing "collagraphs," using collage, varnish, and ink.

In 1995 and 1997, Yvonne won the Oakland Business Arts award for Individual Artist. Her mural work can be seen on 24th Street in San Francisco's Mission District and at the landmark Oakland Hotel.

THE POTTER
Photograph courtesy Yvonne Brown

s	m	t	w	t	f	s
						1
2	3	4	5	6	7	8
9	10	11	12	13	14	15
16	17	18	19	20	21	22
23	24	25	26	27	28	29
30						JUNE

1869: Mary Ellen "Mammy" Pleasant, abolitionist, officially becomes Voodoo Queen in San Francisco.

monday
24 175

1972: Thomas Peters, an African American slave who led black emigrants from Nova Scotia to settle in Sierra Leone, dies.

tuesday
25 176

1993: Roy Campanella, legendary catcher for the Negro leagues and the Los Angeles Dodgers, dies.

wednesday
26 177

1872: Prominent poet and writer Paul Laurence Dunbar is born in Dayton, Ohio.

thursday
27 178

1911: Samuel J. Battle becomes the first African American policeman in New York City.

friday
28 179

1886: Photographer James VanDerZee is born in Lenox, Mass.

saturday
29 180

1917: Actor, vocalist, and civil rights advocate Lena Horne is born in Brooklyn, N.Y.

sunday
30 181

JOHN W. MOSLEY

Born in Lumberton, North Carolina, John W. Mosley (1907–1969) got religion at a very early age. His father was a Baptist minister and barber. John's sister Carolyn, a schoolteacher, influenced him to obtain a strong academic foundation.

Mosley's love for photography began in the 1920s. He learned photographic techniques on the job at the Barksdale Photography Studio. His photographs appeared in every major African American newspaper on the Eastern Seaboard. Mosley's enthusiasm and commitment to his craft served him through nearly four decades. He photographed five U.S. presidents—Roosevelt, Truman, Eisenhower, Kennedy, and Nixon—and scores of prominent actors and actresses, meanwhile documenting the lives of African Americans in Philadelphia. Said one admirer, "Mosley was our most magnificent and our most beloved photographer—he was everywhere." (Excerpted from *The Journey of John W. Mosley: An African-American Pictorial Album*, Temple University Libraries, 1992.)

Photograph by John W. Mosley

Courtesy Charles L. Blockson, African American Collection, Temple University

s	m	t	w	t	f	s
	1	2	3	4	5	6
7	8	9	10	11	12	13
14	15	16	17	18	19	20
21	22	23	24	25	26	27
28	29	30	31			

JULY

CANADA DAY (CANADA)

1899: Rev. Thomas Dorsey, father of gospel music, is born in Villa Rica, Ga.

monday

1 182

1908: Thurgood Marshall, first African American U.S. Supreme Court justice, is born.

tuesday

☾ 2 183

1962: Jackie Robinson is the first African American to be inducted into the National Baseball Hall of Fame.

wednesday

3 184

INDEPENDENCE DAY

1881: Tuskegee Institute opens in Tuskegee, Ala., with Booker T. Washington as its first president.

thursday

4 185

1892: Andrew Beard is issued a patent for the rotary engine.

friday

5 186

1993: Rioters in Lagos, Nigeria, stage an antigovernment protest; eleven lives are lost.

saturday

6 187

1993: Political violence in South Africa continues after declaration of the nation's first all-races democratic election.

sunday

7 188

PIA CALDERON

Born in Mexico City and raised in Rio de Janeiro, Pia Calderon has also lived in Costa Rica and Panama. She currently resides in Maryland with her two sons.

Calderon's paintings reflect her passion for Afro-Brazilian music and the nostalgic *saudades* (love songs) of her childhood. Her work is rooted in the romantic mysticism of Brazilian and Mexican cultures.

After earning an M.F.A. from the University of Maryland, Calderon studied painting with Imogene Cookson at Canal Zone College, where she won three awards from the National Penwomen Association. She usually works in oil, watercolor, and ink.

Of *Rosa Dos Ventos*, she says, "It is a visual rendition of the concept of universe as one image, where the opposites are reconciled in an eternal dance to the music of the spheres. I felt a need for order, to make sense of cyclical nature. My purpose was to create a truly perpetual calendar that is a rose blooming in infinity."

ROSA DOS VENTOS, 1998
Oil on linen

s	m	t	w	t	f	s
	1	2	3	4	5	6
7	8	9	10	11	12	13
14	15	16	17	18	19	20
21	22	23	24	25	26	27
28	29	30	31			

JULY

1943: Women's rights advocate Faye Wattleton is born in St. Louis, Mo.

monday
8 189

1936: Poet and author June Jordan is born in Harlem.

tuesday
9 190

1993: Kenyan runner Yobes Ondieki is the first man to run 10,000 meters in less than 27 minutes.

wednesday
● **10** 191

1915: Mifflin Wistar Gibbs, first African American to be elected a municipal judge, dies.

thursday
11 192

BANK HOLIDAY (N. IRELAND)

1937: William Cosby, Ed.D., comedian, actor, educator, and humanitarian, is born in Philadelphia, Pa.

friday
12 193

1928: Robert N. C. Nix Jr., first African American chief justice of a state supreme court, is born.

saturday
13 194

1996: In Lapeenranta, Finland, Kenyan runner Daniel Komen shaves almost 4 seconds off the world 2-mile record.

sunday
14 195

JULY

DILIP SHETH

Born and raised in Addis Ababa, Ethiopia, Dilip Sheth emigrated to America in 1980. Though he has run a picture-framing business for most of his adult life, his passion is fine art.

Sheth's paintings— images of women caring for their families or hanging out clothes to dry on makeshift clotheslines, scenes of Ethiopian people having coffee (the drink that originated in Ethiopia)—are strongly influenced by his heritage and upbringing.

The painting *Lady in Red* may be Sheth's favorite. He says, "It was inspired by a dream. I love textures in my paintings and *Lady in Red* shows it all. The painting presents a lady very much in control of her surroundings. The walls, abundant with texture, seem to have heard lots of stories. The combination of deep earth tones that dominate the palette and the primitive style are all derived from my early exposure to African art and culture."

LADY IN RED, 1996

Acrylic on paper, 20½ x 20¾ in.

s	m	t	w	t	f	s
	1	2	3	4	5	6
7	8	9	10	11	12	13
14	15	16	17	18	19	20
21	22	23	24	25	26	27
28	29	30	31			

JULY

1929: Francis Bebey, guitarist and author, is born.

monday

15 196

1822: Violette A. Johnson, first African American woman to practice before the U.S. Supreme Court, is born.

tuesday

16 197

1911: Frank Snowden, foremost scholar on Africans in ancient history, is born in York County, Va.

wednesday

☽ **17** 198

1899: L. C. Bailey is issued a patent for the folding bed.

thursday

18 199

1979: In her second Cabinet-level appointment, Patricia Roberts Harris is named secretary of the U.S. Department of Health and Human Services.

friday

19 200

1967: The first National Conference of Black Power opens in Newark, N.J.

saturday

20 201

1896: Mary Church Terrell founds the National Association of Colored Women in Washington, D.C.

sunday

21 202

MARGARET JUST BUTCHER

Margaret Just Butcher is the eldest daughter of zoologist Ernest Just and educator Ethel Highwarden—professionals who instilled in their children a strong belief in the power of achievement through education. Butcher (b. 1913) traveled abroad, attended school in Italy and at Emerson College, and received a doctoral degree from Boston University in 1947. Heeding her parents' advice, she became an educator; Butcher taught at Virginia Union University, Howard University, and Federal City College as well as in the Washington, D.C., public schools. Throughout her career, Butcher remained a strong advocate for equality in education.

Butcher is best known for her association with Alain Locke, the Harlem Renaissance philosopher and educator and a close friend of her father. Just before Locke's death in 1954, she was entrusted with his research materials for a major unfinished book, *The Negro in American Culture*. At Locke's request, Butcher completed this important work.

Photograph courtesy National Archives

s	m	t	w	t	f	s
	1	2	3	4	5	6
7	8	9	10	11	12	13
14	15	16	17	18	19	20
21	22	23	24	25	26	27
28	29	30	31			

JULY

1939: Jane Bolin is appointed to the Domestic Relations Court, becoming the first female African American judge.

monday
22 203

1868: The 14th Amendment is ratified, granting citizenship to African Americans.

tuesday
23 204

1925: Operatic soprano Adele Addison is born in New York City.

wednesday
○ **24** 205

1916: Wearing the protective mask he invented, Garrett Morgan enters a gas-filled tunnel with a rescue party after an underground explosion in Cleveland, Ohio; six lives are saved.

thursday
25 206

1865: Catholic priest Patrick Francis Healy becomes the first African American to earn a Ph.D. degree.

friday
26 207

1996: Duncan Bailey, a Jamaican running for Canada, becomes the "world's fastest human" by completing the 100-meter run in 9.84 seconds in the Atlanta Olympics.

saturday
27 208

1996: Ethiopian police officer Fatuma Roba is the first African woman to win a medal in an Olympic marathon.

sunday
28 209

LOU STOVALL

A master printmaker and teacher, Lou Stovall has made prints of more than eighty artists, including Sam Gilliam, Elizabeth Catlett, Loïs Mailou Jones, Jacob Lawrence, Robert Mangold, and Peter Blume.

In a treatise on printmaking, Stovall wrote the following:

"Silkscreen printing has long been an established method of creating fine art, and in collaboration with a master printmaker, the process is available to artists from a broad range of mediums. . . . Silkscreen prints are made by direct impression through the silk; because of this, colors may be built up in much the same manner that paintings are made. While I strive to make each silkscreen print look like its original medium, I am always open to even the whim of an artist to try something a little different.

"Fascination with the sheer beauty of silk-screened ink on paper will probably last forever. It begins with color, the single most compelling element in silkscreen printmaking."

HEART III

Silkscreen, 8¼ x 8¼ in.

Courtesy Lou Stovall

s	m	t	w	t	f	s
					1	2	3
4	5	6	7	8	9	10
11	12	13	14	15	16	17
18	19	20	21	22	23	24
25	26	27	28	29	30	31

AUGUST

1909: Crime novelist Chester Himes is born in Jefferson City, Mo.

monday
29 210

1996: Three years after recovering from third-degree burns, Cuba's Ana Quirot wins a silver medal in the 800-meter run in the Atlanta Olympics.

tuesday
30 211

1921: Educator and civil rights activist Whitney Young Jr. is born in Lincoln Ridge, Ky.

wednesday
31 212

1996: Michael Johnson is the first man to win gold medals in both the 200- and 400-meter runs, breaking his own world record.

thursday
☽ **1** 213

1847: William A. Leidesdorff launches the first steamboat in San Francisco Bay.

friday
2 214

1996: Josia Thugwane is the first black South African to win an Olympic gold medal, completing the marathon in 2 hours, 12 minutes, 36 seconds.

saturday
3 215

1875: The Convention of Colored Newspapermen is held in Cincinnati, Ohio.

sunday
4 216

AUGUST

DR. CLAUDIA LYNN THOMAS

Dr. Claudia Lynn Thomas, assistant professor of orthopedics at Johns Hopkins University School of Medicine, is the first black woman orthopedic surgeon in the country. Born in New York, she studied at Vassar and Johns Hopkins, completing her residency in orthopedics at Yale.

Dr. Thomas has experienced a life-threatening ailment. In 1990, her kidneys were found to be cancerous and were removed. She spent the next five years on dialysis until she underwent a kidney transplant. "I am proud of my physical survival and the faith in God that it has reinstilled in me," she says.

Dr. Thomas is active in the Baltimore community, speaking in schools to encourage students to continue their education. Largely through her efforts, Johns Hopkins has increased numbers of women and minorities in the orthopedics department. Thomas says, "You have to believe that God's going to get you through it. If you can believe it, you can overcome anything. Just see the obstacles as opportunities."

Photograph by Linda M. King

Courtesy Dr. Claudia Thomas and
 Labors of Love

s	m	t	w	t	f	s
					1	2	3
4	5	6	7	8	9	10
11	12	13	14	15	16	17
18	19	20	21	22	23	24
25	26	27	28	29	30	31

AUGUST

BANK HOLIDAY (SCOTLAND)

1914: The first electric traffic lights (invented by Garrett Morgan) are installed at Euclid Ave. and 105th St., Cleveland, Ohio.

monday
5 217

1965: President Lyndon B. Johnson signs the Voting Rights Act, outlawing the literacy test for voting eligibility in the South.

tuesday
6 218

1904: Ralph Bunche, first African American Nobel Prize winner, is born in Detroit, Mich.

wednesday
7 219

1865: Matthew A. Henson, first explorer to reach the North Pole, is born in Charles County, Md.

thursday
8 220

1936: Jesse Owens wins four gold medals in track and field events at the Berlin Olympics.

friday
9 221

1989: Gen. Colin Powell is nominated as chairman of the Joint Chiefs of Staff.

saturday
10 222

1921: Alex Haley, author, is born in Ithaca, N.Y.

sunday
11 223

PATRICK HEALY

Patrick Healy (1834–1910) is believed to be the first U.S. black to earn a Ph.D. He was born to Michael Healy, a transplanted Irishman, and Mary Eliza, a former slave; according to Georgia law, their children could have been sold as slaves. In fact, a group of white planters once suggested that the Healys do just that; Michael Healy sicced his dogs on them. Thereafter, the parents dedicated themselves to providing education and opportunity for their children.

Patrick became the first black president of Georgetown University in Washington, D.C. Father Healy led Georgetown through a period of growth following the Civil War. One of his accomplishments was the construction of the magnificent Healy Building. Completed in 1877, it still dominates Georgetown's skyline. The building, designed in the Flemish Renaissance style reminiscent of the architecture Healy admired when he studied in Europe, is a lasting reminder of his outstanding leadership.

Photograph courtesy Georgetown
    University Archives

s	m	t	w	t	f	s
					1	2	3
4	5	6	7	8	9	10
11	12	13	14	15	16	17
18	19	20	21	22	23	24
25	26	27	28	29	30	31

AUGUST

1977: Steven Biko, leader of the black consciousness movement in South Africa, is arrested.

monday
12 224

1989: The wreckage of the plane that carried U.S. Congressman Mickey Leland and others on a humanitarian mission is found on a mountainside in Ethiopia; there are no survivors.

tuesday
13 225

1990: Singer Curtis Mayfield is paralyzed in an accident at an outdoor concert in Brooklyn, N.Y.

wednesday
14 226

1938: Maxine Waters, second African American woman from California to be elected to Congress, is born.

thursday
☽ **15** 227

1938: Innovative blues guitarist Robert Johnson dies in Greenwood, Miss.

friday
16 228

1993: Jackie Joyner-Kersee wins her seventeenth consecutive heptathlon, edging out Germany's Sabine Braun in the World Track and Field Championships in Stuttgart, Germany.

saturday
17 229

1963: James Meredith becomes the first African American to graduate from the Univ. of Mississippi.

sunday
18 230

AUGUST

FLEMMIE KITTRELL

Flemmie Kittrell (1904–1980) was one of America's leading advocates of nutritional education. As a representative of the U.S. government, she traveled throughout Africa, India, and other developing countries, educating people about nutrition.

Born in Henderson, North Carolina, Kittrell graduated from the Hampton Normal and Agricultural Institute in Virginia, then became head of the Department of Home Economics at Howard University in Washington, D.C. There she emphasized the importance of research and long-term studies in determining a community's nutritional needs. In 1950, helping to develop the home economics department at Baroda University in India, Kittrell taught courses in food and nutrition, meal planning, and child feeding. She undertook similar projects in Africa, Japan, and Hawaii.

On returning to the United States, Kittrell focused on improving Howard University's home economics department. Through her efforts, the School of Human Ecology building was constructed. Kittrell remained on the staff there until her retirement in 1972.

Photograph courtesy Bethune Museum and Archives

s	m	t	w	t	f	s
					1	2	3
4	5	6	7	8	9	10
11	12	13	14	15	16	17
18	19	20	21	22	23	24
25	26	27	28	29	30	31

AUGUST

1989: Bishop Desmond Tutu defies apartheid laws by walking alone on a South African beach.

monday
19 231

1619: The first group of 20 Africans is brought to Jamestown, Va.

tuesday
20 232

1904: Bandleader and composer William "Count" Basie is born in Red Bank, N.J.

wednesday
21 233

1978: Kenyan president and revolutionary Jomo Kenyatta dies.

thursday
○ **22** 234

1900: Booker T. Washington forms the National Negro Business League in Boston, Mass.

friday
23 235

1948: Edith Mae Irby becomes the Univ. of Arkansas' first African American student.

saturday
24 236

1989: Huey P. Newton, cofounder of the Black Panther Party, dies.

sunday
25 237

AUG/SEPT

Dr. Ivan Van Sertima

Born in British Guyana in 1935, Ivan Van Sertima studied in England and eventually immigrated to the United States. An early incident spurred his interest in acquiring knowledge. After hearing the term *negro* applied to him and other blacks, young Ivan consulted a leading encyclopedia for a definition of the word. The entry included the statement that "after adolescence the sutures in the crania of the Negro become calcified, making the brain non-functional, and the Negro unable to retain information and learn." Van Sertima remembers: "I became obsessed with reading and studying anything and everything I could before my brain would close down."

Dr. Van Sertima, currently a professor of African studies at Rutgers University, is best known for *They Came Before Columbus: The African Presence in Ancient America* (1977). In this book, Van Sertima presents groundbreaking research revealing an ancient African presence in the Americas.

Photograph by Jacqueline L. Patten–Van Sertima

s	m	t	w	t	f	s
1	2	3	4	5	6	7
8	9	10	11	12	13	14
15	16	17	18	19	20	21
22	23	24	25	26	27	28
29	30					

SEPTEMBER

BANK HOLIDAY (U.K. EXCEPT SCOTLAND)

1946: Composer, singer, and producer Valerie Simpson Ashford is born.

monday
26 238

1963: W. E. B. Du Bois, scholar, civil rights activist, and founding father of the NAACP, dies in Accra, Ghana.

tuesday
27 239

1963: Largest single demonstration in the history of the United States, the March on Washington for Jobs and Freedom, takes place.

wednesday
28 240

1920: Jazz saxophonist Charlie "Bird" Parker is born in Kansas City, Kans.

thursday
29 241

1983: Lt. Col. Guion S. Bluford Jr. is the first African American in space.

friday
30 242

1935: Baseball player and manager Frank Robinson is born in Beaufort, Tex.

saturday
☾ **31** 243

1993: Soviet military expert Condoleeza Rice is named provost at Stanford Univ., becoming the youngest person and the first black to hold this position.

sunday
1 244

FANNIE JACKSON COPPIN

Born a slave, Fannie Jackson Coppin (1836–1913) was virtually self-educated. Prominent white families who noticed her exceptional intellect welcomed her into their homes, providing her with room and board and the opportunity to study. She eventually attended Oberlin College, mastered Latin, Greek, and mathematics, and graduated in 1865.

Coppin was committed to educating the newly freed black people—and to dispelling the myth that they were intellectually inferior. She became a teacher at the Quakers Institute for Colored Youth. During one of her classes, she asked an Englishman to take over the class and observe her students. He commented afterward: "They are more capable of examining me. Their proficiency is wonderful." Coppin State College in Baltimore, Maryland, is named after her.

Photograph courtesy the African American Museum and Library at Oakland

s	m	t	w	t	f	s
1	2	3	4	5	6	7
8	9	10	11	12	13	14
15	16	17	18	19	20	21
22	23	24	25	26	27	28
29	30					

SEPTEMBER

LABOR DAY (U.S., CANADA)

monday
2 245

1975: Joseph W. Hatcher of Tallahassee, Fla., becomes the state's first African American supreme court justice since Reconstruction.

---

tuesday
3 246

1838: Frederick Douglass escapes from slavery, disguised as a sailor.

---

wednesday
4 247

1957: Arkansas governor Orval Faubus calls out the National Guard to bar African American students from entering a Little Rock high school.

---

thursday
5 248

1960: Leopold Sedar Senghor, poet and politician, is elected president of Senegal.

ROSH HASHANAH (BEGINS AT SUNSET)

friday
6 249

1996: Eddie Murray of the Baltimore Orioles joins Hank Aaron and Willie Mays as the only baseball players with at least 500 home runs and 3,000 hits.

---

saturday
7 250

1954: Integration of public schools begins in Washington, D.C., and Baltimore, Md.

---

sunday
8 251

1981: Roy Wilkins, executive director of the NAACP, dies.

SEPTEMBER

P. B. S. PINCHBACK

Pinckney Benton Stewart Pinchback (1837–1921) was born to Mississippi farmer William Pinchback and his former slave Eliza Stewart. After his father's death, Pinchback worked on canalboats and riverboats to help support his family.

When the Civil War erupted, Pinchback joined the Union forces and recruited blacks into a regiment known as the Corps d'Afrique. He soon resigned to protest discriminatory treatment of his troops, stating, "If they were not allowed to vote, they should not be drafted. My troops did not ask for social equality and did not expect it, but they demanded political rights—they wanted to be men."

In 1872, he served as acting governor during the elected governor's impeachment proceedings. In a heavily contested election, Pinchback was chosen by the state legislature to serve in the state senate. Pinchback was a friend and supporter of Booker T. Washington, and in 1898 he participated in the unveiling of the Frederick Douglass monument in Rochester, New York.

Photograph courtesy Library of Congress

s	m	t	w	t	f	s
1	2	3	4	5	6	7
8	9	10	11	12	13	14
15	16	17	18	19	20	21
22	23	24	25	26	27	28
29	30					

SEPTEMBER

1915: Dr. Carter G. Woodson founds the Association for the Study of Negro Life and History.

monday

9 252

1961: Jomo Kenyatta returns to Kenya from exile, during which he had been elected president of the Kenya National African Union.

tuesday

10 253

1974: Haile Selassie I is deposed from the Ethiopian throne.

wednesday

11 254

1913: Track and field star Jesse Owens is born in Oakville, Ala.

thursday

12 255

1971: New York state troopers crush a revolt at Attica State Prison; twenty-eight inmates and nine hostages are killed.

friday

☽ **13** 256

1980: Dorothy Boulding Ferebee, physician and second president of the National Council for Negro Women, dies.

saturday

14 257

YOM KIPPUR (BEGINS AT SUNSET)

1943: Paul Robeson performs in *Othello* for the 269th time.

sunday

15 258

MIRIAM ZENZI MAKEBA

Sekou Toure, former president of Guinea, called Miriam Makeba "the Empress of African Song." This is surely an apt title, for only an empress could have graced the international stage for so many world leaders—including Jomo Kenyatta, Haile Selassie, Fidel Castro, François Mitterand, and John Kennedy—with such style.

While her music was banned in her homeland, South Africa, from 1960 to 1990, Makeba became a citizen of the world. In 1962, she addressed the United Nations Special Committee on Apartheid. In 1967, her song "Pata Pata" became a worldwide hit. Makeba was awarded the Dag Hammarskjold Peace Prize in 1986. In 1995, she performed in Italy for Pope John Paul II and toured Germany, Austria, the United States, and Australia. At the invitation of President Ben Ali of Tunisia, she performed at the Carthage Music Festival.

Miriam Makeba is an inspiration for the youth of her own country, and through her music she has touched the hearts and consciences of people around the world.

Photograph courtesy National Archives

s	m	t	w	t	f	s
1	2	3	4	5	6	7
8	9	10	11	12	13	14
15	16	17	18	19	20	21
22	23	24	25	26	27	28
29	30					

SEPTEMBER

1925: Blues great B. B. King is born in Indianola, Miss.

monday
16 259

1983: Vanessa Williams, Miss New York, becomes the first black Miss America.

tuesday
17 260

1980: Cosmonaut Arnoldo Tamayo, a Cuban, becomes the first black to travel in space.

wednesday
18 261

1989: Gordon Parks's film *The Learning Tree* is among the first films to be registered by the National Film Registry of the Library of Congress.

thursday
19 262

1830: The National Negro Convention convenes in Philadelphia with the purpose of abolishing slavery.

friday
20 263

1982: Players begin an eight-week strike against all twenty-eight NFL teams, cutting short the fall season.

saturday
○ **21** 264

1915: Xavier Univ., the first African American Catholic college, opens in New Orleans, La.

sunday
22 265

SEPTEMBER

JOSEPH BOULOGNE
ST. GEORGES

For much of the eighteenth century, European culture took its cues from France. With revolution still on the horizon, the French elite were masters of music, painting, dance, literature, and drama.

Joseph Boulogne Saint-Georges was born on the Caribbean island of Guadeloupe to an African slave mother and a French father. Saint-Georges (1739–1799) and his family settled in Paris in 1749. At thirteen Saint-Georges began studying fencing under the "master of arms" La Boessiere, the same instructor who taught Saint-Georges' friend Thomas-Alexandre Dumas. Focusing primarily on physical training and academic studies in his early school years, Saint-Georges became a proficient violin player, quickly learning composition by playing his own music.

A prolific composer, Saint-Georges created eleven symphonies, several operas, twelve string quartets, ten violin concertos, and other instrumental and vocal works. He was also an expert swordsman, swimmer, and boxer, and colonel of an all-black regiment during the revolution.

Photograph courtesy IOKTS Archives

s	m	t	w	t	f	s
1	2	3	4	5	6	7
8	9	10	11	12	13	14
15	16	17	18	19	20	21
22	23	24	25	26	27	28
29	30					

SEPTEMBER

AUTUMNAL EQUINOX 4:56 A.M. (GMT)

1993: South Africa's parliament creates a multiracial body to oversee the end of exclusive white control of the nation.

monday
23 266

1923: Nancy Green, the world's first living trademark (Aunt Jemima), is struck and killed by an automobile in Chicago.

tuesday
24 267

1974: Barbara W. Hancock is the first African American woman to be named a White House Fellow.

wednesday
25 268

1937: Bessie Smith, "Empress of the Blues," dies.

thursday
26 269

1944: Stephanie Pogue, artist and art professor, is born in Shelby, N.C.

friday
27 270

1912: W. C. Handy's "Memphis Blues" is published.

saturday
28 271

1980: The Schomburg Center for Research in Black Culture opens a new $3.8 million building in New York City.

sunday
☾ 29 272

MARY CHURCH TERRELL

She came from an affluent family and was light skinned enough to "pass" as a white person. Instead, Mary Church Terrell (1863–1954) placed herself squarely in the struggle for African American empowerment and achieved a lifetime of accomplishments in education, social service, and politics.

Terrell taught at Wilberforce University in Ohio, then moved to secondary school teaching in Washington, D.C. Her later appointment to the District of Columbia Board of Education was a first for an African American woman. As the first president of the Colored Women's League of Washington and later as president of the National Association of Colored Women, Terrell was instrumental in local affiliates' establishment of kindergartens, day care centers, and nursing schools. She joined Frederick Douglass in pushing for antilynching measures, and after his death continued to pursue the cause of woman suffrage. Terrell was a pioneer in attacking segregation in Washington. Her motto: "Keep on going, keep on insisting, keep on fighting injustice."

Photograph courtesy National Archives for Black Women's History

s	m	t	w	t	f	s
		1	2	3	4	5
6	7	8	9	10	11	12
13	14	15	16	17	18	19
20	21	22	23	24	25	26
27	28	29	30	31		

OCTOBER

1935: Singer Johnny Mathis is born in San Francisco, Calif.

monday

30 273

1996: Lt. Gen. Joe Ballard becomes the first African American to head the Army Corps of Engineers.

tuesday

1 274

1958: The Republic of Guinea gains independence under Sekou Toure.

wednesday

2 275

1990: Rio de Janeiro's first black congresswoman, Benedita da Silva, sweeps the first round of the city's mayoral race.

thursday

3 276

1943: H. Rap Brown, chairman of the Student Nonviolent Coordinating Committee (SNCC), is born.

friday

4 277

1878: George B. Vashon, first African American lawyer in the state of New York, dies in Rodney, Miss.

saturday

5 278

1917: Fannie Lou Hamer, founder of the Mississippi Freedom Democratic Party, is born in Montgomery County, Miss.

sunday

● **6** 279

OCTOBER

MADAME LILLIAN EVANTI

In the 1920s, she was the first African American to develop a professional career in grand opera. Later, Lillian Evanti (1890–1967), born Lillian Evans, became a celebrated concert artist and an advocate of civil and cultural rights. Born in Washington, D.C., Evans received her B.S. in music from Howard University. She later married her teacher, Roy Wilfred Tibbs, professor of music at Howard from 1914 to 1944. Harlem Renaissance writer Jesse Fauset suggested that the name Evanti is a contraction of Evans and Tibbs, giving Madame Lillian an Italianate name.

One highlight of Evanti's career was a 1940 tour of Argentina and Brazil with Arturo Toscanini and the NBC Orchestra. In the fifties, she made several concert tours to Africa, where she was decorated for her cultural contributions in Nigeria, Liberia, and Ghana. In 1957 Evanti wrote Ghana's independence song.

An ardent civil and human rights activist, Lillian Evanti supported full "home rule" for the District of Columbia.

Photograph courtesy Evans–Tibbs Collection

s	m	t	w	t	f	s
		1	2	3	4	5
6	7	8	9	10	11	12
13	14	15	16	17	18	19
20	21	22	23	24	25	26
27	28	29	30	31		

OCTOBER

1993: Author Toni Morrison is the first African American to win the Nobel Prize in literature.

monday
7 280

1941: Rev. Jesse L. Jackson, political activist and civil rights leader, is born in Greenville, S.C.

tuesday
8 281

1806: Mathematician and astronomer Benjamin Banneker dies in Ellicott City, Md.

wednesday
9 282

1901: Frederick Douglass Patterson, founder of the United Negro College Fund, is born.

thursday
10 283

1919: Jazz drummer and bandleader Art Blakey is born in Pittsburgh, Pa.

friday
11 284

COLUMBUS DAY

1932: Comedian and civil rights activist Dick Gregory is born in St. Louis, Mo.

saturday
12 285

1902: Arna Bontemps, poet and librarian, is born in Alexandria, La.

sunday
☽ **13** 286

OCTOBER

LANGSTON HUGHES

Langston Hughes was popularly known as the Poet Laureate of Harlem. Among the most prolific and versatile twentieth-century literary artists, Hughes (1902–1967) wrote poetry, dramas, short stories, novels, librettos, children's stories, speeches, and biographies. He was one of the most important writers of the Harlem Renaissance, producing such collections of poetry as *The Weary Blues* (1926), *Fine Clothes to the Jew* (1927), *Dear Lovely Death* (1931), and *The Dream-Keeper and Other Poems* (1932). Other well-known works include the novel *Not Without Laughter* (1930), the short-story collection *The Ways of White Folks* (1934), the play *Mulatto* (1935), and the poetry collection *Shakespeare in Harlem* (1942).

Hughes received the Harmon Award in 1930, and in 1935 traveled to Russia and Spain on a Guggenheim Fellowship.

Photograph courtesy Library of Congress

COLUMBUS DAY OBSERVED
THANKSGIVING DAY (CANADA)

monday
14 287

1964: Dr. Martin Luther King Jr. is awarded the Nobel Peace Prize.

1968: Wyomia Tyus becomes the first person to win a gold medal in the 100-meter race in two consecutive Olympic games.

tuesday
15 288

1995: The Million Man March, for "A Day of Atonement," takes place in Washington, D.C.

wednesday
16 289

1806: Jean-Jacques Dessalines, revolutionist and emperor of Haiti, is assassinated.

thursday
17 290

1926: Rock 'n' roll legend Chuck Berry is born in St. Louis, Mo.

friday
18 291

1878: Dr. Frederick Victor Nanka Bruce, the first physician on the Gold Coast, is born in Accra, Ghana.

saturday
19 292

---

s	m	t	w	t	f	s
		1	2	3	4	5
6	7	8	9	10	11	12
13	14	15	16	17	18	19
20	21	22	23	24	25	26
27	28	29	30	31		

OCTOBER

1989: Federal judge Alcee L. Hastings is impeached by the U.S. Senate.

sunday
20 293

OCTOBER

PATRICIA ROBERTS HARRIS

Commitment to public service and pioneering personal achievement are the foundation on which Patricia Roberts Harris (1924–1985)—attorney, ambassador, and Cabinet member—built her life. Born in Mattoon, Illinois, Harris graduated *summa cum laude* from Howard University, where she cochaired the NAACP's student chapter.

In 1960, after graduating with honors from Washington University's law school, Harris was admitted to practice before the U.S. Supreme Court and the District of Columbia bar. Always a political activist and civil rights advocate, she was appointed to the National Women's Committee on Civil Rights by President John F. Kennedy.

Harris's commitment to quality education, government by and for the people, and social reform based on justice crystalized in 1977, when President Jimmy Carter appointed her Secretary of Housing and Urban Development. The first African American woman to hold a cabinet-level position, Harris went on to become Secretary of Health and Human Services in 1979.

Photograph courtesy Bethune Museum

s	m	t	w	t	f	s
		1	2	3	4	5
6	7	8	9	10	11	12
13	14	15	16	17	18	19
20	21	22	23	24	25	26
27	28	29	30	31		

OCTOBER

1872: John H. Conyers Sr. is the first African American to be admitted to the U.S. Naval Academy.

monday
21 294

1936: Bobby Seale, cofounder of the Black Panther Party, is born in Dallas, Tex.

tuesday
22 295

1886: Wiley Jones operates the first streetcar in Pine Bluff, Ark.

wednesday
23 296

UNITED NATIONS DAY
1996: Robert M. Bell is the first African American to serve as chief judge of Maryland's Court of Appeals.

thursday
24 297

1992: Vivian Dandridge, dancer and sister of actor Dorothy Dandridge, dies.

friday
25 298

1962: Actor Louise Beavers dies in Los Angeles.

saturday
26 299

DAYLIGHT SAVING TIME ENDS
SUMMER TIME ENDS (U.K.)
1891: D. B. Downing, inventor, is awarded a patent for the street letter box.

sunday
27 300

OCT/NOV

OSCEOLA

The Seminole Indians comprised refugees from devastated Southeastern tribes and runaway black slaves who settled in central Florida. According to historians, "Seminole" means "pioneer" or "one who secedes." It is also said to be a corruption of the Spanish word *cimmaron*—"wild."

In the 1830s, Osceola (1804–1838) led the Seminoles' fight against the United States government's efforts to relocate them. The United States spent $50 million and the lives of more than 2,000 soldiers. The Seminoles lost more.

In October 1837, while negotiating under a flag of truce, Osceola was taken prisoner. His imprisonment attracted national attention, and the famed artist George Catlin obtained a commission from the War Department to paint his portrait. Catlin observed: "Osceola is a most extraordinary man . . . a cunning and restless spirit."

Between 1835 and 1842, more than four thousand Seminoles were forcibly relocated to the Indian Territories, in what is now eastern Oklahoma.

Courtesy National Archives

s	m	t	w	t	f	s
					1	2
3	4	5	6	7	8	9
10	11	12	13	14	15	16
17	18	19	20	21	22	23
24	25	26	27	28	29	30

NOVEMBER

1873–1879: Patrick Healy serves as president of Georgetown University, the oldest Catholic university in the United States.

monday
28 301

1949: Alonzo G. Moron of the Virgin Islands becomes the first African American president of Hampton Institute, Va.

tuesday
29 302

1829: David Walker, a freeborn black, is the first to oppose slavery through the press.

wednesday
30 303

HALLOWEEN
1900: Actor and singer Ethel Waters is born in Chester, Pa.

thursday
31 304

1945: John H. Johnson publishes the first issue of *Ebony.*

friday
1 305

1983: President Ronald Reagan signs a law designating the third Monday in January as Martin Luther King Jr. Day.

saturday
2 306

1983: Jesse Jackson announces his candidacy for the office of president of the United States.

sunday
3 307

NOVEMBER

EDITH SAMPSON

Born in Pittsburgh, Edith Spurlock Sampson (1901–1979) learned early about survival and the importance of earning and saving money. Realizing that education was her ticket out of poverty, and wanting to help others, she became a lawyer and served the Cook County, Illinois, juvenile court while maintaining a private practice. Sampson became a leading Chicago attorney, hurdling the barriers that kept women and blacks out of the field of jurisprudence.

In 1962, Sampson became the first black woman in American history to be elected a judge. Sampson was also the first woman to graduate from the Loyola University Law School in Chicago, the first black delegate to the United Nations, and the first black person to hold an appointment with NATO.

In speaking about equality for blacks in America she stated, "When we Negroes achieve first-class citizenship in America, we will not drape our mantles over our shoulders and return anywhere; we are already there."

Photograph courtesy National Archives for Black Women's History

s	m	t	w	t	f	s
					1	2
3	4	5	6	7	8	9
10	11	12	13	14	15	16
17	18	19	20	21	22	23
24	25	26	27	28	29	30

NOVEMBER

1992: Carol Moseley Braun is the first African American woman to be elected to the U.S. Senate.

monday

4 308

ELECTION DAY
1862: Frazier A. Boutelle is commissioned as second lieutenant in the Fifth New York Cavalry.

tuesday

5 309

1989: Renowned attorney Sadie Tanner Mossell Alexander dies in Philadelphia, Pa.

wednesday

6 310

1989: Douglas Wilder becomes the nation's first black governor (Virginia) since Reconstruction.

thursday

7 311

1938: Crystal Bird Fauset of Pennsylvania is the first African American woman to be elected to a state legislature.

friday

8 312

1731: Benjamin Banneker, inventor of the first wooden clock in America, is born in Ellicott City, Md.

saturday

9 313

1995: Nigerian author and poet Ken Saro-Wiwa is executed.

sunday

10 314

NOVEMBER

COLONEL CHARLES YOUNG

Born in Mays Lick, Kentucky, Colonel Charles Young (1864–1922) attended the U.S. Military Academy at West Point in 1884. Though he was ostracized because of racial prejudice, he persevered, graduating on August 31, 1889. Young's military career began when blacks had recently been allowed to serve but were still restricted to all-black regiments. During the Spanish-American War, the black regiments in the 24th Cavalry earned respect when they rescued Theodore Roosevelt's "rough riders" at San Juan Hiill. Young, in charge of the Ninth Ohio Regiment, advanced to become the highest-ranking black in the U.S. Army in 1918.

In 1919, Young was appointed military attaché to the U.S. embassy in Liberia, where he helped reorganize Liberian forces during that country's difficult adjustment to independence. He died while on a research expedition to Lagos, Nigeria.

Photograph courtesy African American Museum and Library at Oakland

s	m	t	w	t	f	s
					1	2
3	4	5	6	7	8	9
10	11	12	13	14	15	16
17	18	19	20	21	22	23
24	25	26	27	28	29	30

NOVEMBER

VETERANS' DAY
REMEMBRANCE DAY (CANADA)
1989: The Civil Rights Memorial in Montgomery, Ala., is dedicated.

monday
☽ 11 315

1941: Madame Lillian Evanti and Mary Cardwell Dawson establish the National Negro Opera Company.

tuesday
12 316

1940: U.S. Supreme Court rules in *Hansberry v. Lee* that African Americans cannot be barred from white neighborhoods.

wednesday
13 317

1954: Dr. James Joshua Thomas is installed as minister of the Mott Haven Reformed Church in The Bronx, N.Y.

thursday
14 318

218 B.C.: Hannibal crosses the Alps with elephants and 26,000 men to defeat Roman troops at the Ticino and Trebbia Rivers.

friday
15 319

1873: W. C. Handy, father of the blues, is born in Florence, Ala.

saturday
16 320

1980: WHMM-TV in Washington, D.C., becomes the first African American public broadcasting television station.

sunday
17 321

NOVEMBER

WILLA BROWN

Willa Brown is one of a group of flyers responsible for creating interest among blacks in aviation, particularly in the Chicago area. Her résumé includes a number of aviation firsts: she was the first black woman to hold a commercial pilot's license, the first black member of the Illinois Civil Air Patrol, and the first black woman to make a career of aviation.

Born in Glasgow, Kentucky, in 1906, Brown attended high school in Terre Haute, Indiana, and later graduated from Indiana Teachers College with degrees in business and French. She eventually moved to Chicago, where she met two pioneering aviators—Cornelius Coffey (whom she would later marry) and John Robinson, who encouraged her to fly. After Brown received her commercial pilot's license, aviation became the central focus of her life. Brown and Coffey directed a successful flight training school under the government-sponsored Civil Pilot Training Program. More than two hundred pilots earned their wings under Brown's tutelage.

Photograph courtesy National Archives

s	m	t	w	t	f	s
					1	2
3	4	5	6	7	8	9
10	11	12	13	14	15	16
17	18	19	20	21	22	23
24	25	26	27	28	29	30

NOVEMBER

1900: Dr. Howard Thurman, theologian and first African American to hold a full-time position at Boston Univ., is born.

monday
18 322

1797: Abolitionist and women's rights advocate Sojourner Truth is born in New York.

tuesday
19 323

1695: Zumbi dos Palmares, Brazilian leader of a hundred-year-old rebel slave group, is killed in an ambush.

wednesday
○ **20** 324

1866: Duse Mohammed Effendi, Egyptian Pan-Africanist, is born.

thursday
21 325

1994: Jazz musicians Herbie Hancock, Clark Terry, and Joshua Redman perform in a concert beamed by satellite to sixty schools nationwide.

friday
22 326

1941: Musician and actor Henrietta Vinton Davis dies in Washington, D.C.

saturday
23 327

1868: Scott Joplin, originator of ragtime music, is born in Texarkana, Tex.

sunday
24 328

NOV/DEC

GUION BLUFORD

On August 30, 1983, "Guy" Bluford became the first black American to go into space. Born in Philadelphia, Bluford graduated from Overbrook Senior High School. He received his B.S. Degree from Penn State, an M.S. from the Air Force Institute of Technology, and a Ph.D in aerospace engineering (with a minor in laser physics) from the institute in 1978.

Bluford earned his wings in 1965; he has logged over 3,500 hours of flying time in jets, including 1,300 hours as an instructor. Bluford first served as a mission specialist on STS-8 (the orbiter *Challenger.*) His next mission was on STS 61-A, the German Spacelab mission. This flight had the largest crew to fly in space (eight). His third mission, giving him a total of 513 hours in space, was aboard the orbiter *Discovery* on April 28, 1991. After completing 134 orbits of the earth, *Discovery* landed at the Kennedy Space Center on May 6, 1991.

Photograph courtesy NASA

s	m	t	w	t	f	s
1	2	3	4	5	6	7
8	9	10	11	12	13	14
15	16	17	18	19	20	21
22	23	24	25	26	27	28
29	30	31				

DECEMBER

1955: The Interstate Commerce Commission bans segregation in interstate travel.

monday 25 329

1866: Rust College is founded in Holly Springs, Miss.

tuesday 26 330

1942: Rock musician Jimi Hendrix is born in Seattle, Wash.

wednesday ☾ 27 331

THANKSGIVING DAY
1961: Ernie Davis is the first African American to win the Heisman Trophy.

thursday 28 332

HANUKKAH (BEGINS AT SUNSET)
1908: Adam Clayton Powell Jr., politician and civil rights activist, is born in New Haven, Conn.

friday 29 333

FIRST DAY OF HANUKKAH
1912: Gordon Parks, filmmaker and photographer, is born.

saturday 30 334

1955: Rosa Parks defies the segregated transportation ordinance in Montgomery, Ala., igniting a 382-day bus boycott and launching the civil rights movement in America.

sunday 1 335

DECEMBER

STEPHANIE WILSON

An astronaut in the making, Stephanie Wilson was born in 1966 in Boston. She graduated from Taconic High School and received a BS in engineering science from Harvard in 1988. After graduating, she worked for two years for the Martin Marietta Astronautics Group in Denver, Colorado, then attended graduate school at the University of Texas. Her graduate research involved studying the means to control and model large, flexible space structures. Upon completion of this work, Wilson went to work at the Jet Propulsion Laboratory in Pasadena, California. There she was responsible for assessing attitude controller performance, science platform pointing accuracy, antenna pointing accuracy, and spin rate accuracy for the *Galileo* spacecraft.

NASA selected Stephanie Wilson in 1996. After completing two years of training and evaluation, she is qualified for flight assignment as a mission specialist. She is currently assigned to technical duties in the Astronaut Office Space Station Operations Branch.

Photograph courtesy NASA

s	m	t	w	t	f	s
1	2	3	4	5	6	7
8	9	10	11	12	13	14
15	16	17	18	19	20	21
22	23	24	25	26	27	28
29	30	31				

DECEMBER

1968: Dial Press publishes Frank Yerby's *Judas My Brother*.

monday
2 336

1911: Distinguished educator and historian Helen Gray Edmonds is born in Lawrenceville, Va.

tuesday
3 337

1906: Alpha Phi Alpha Fraternity is founded at Cornell Univ., the first African American Greek organization to be chartered.

wednesday
● **4** 338

1870: Alexandre Dumas (père), French novelist and dramatist, dies.

thursday
5 339

1960: Some five hundred store owners in Tucson, Ariz., sign pledges vowing not to discriminate on the basis of race, color, or religion.

friday
6 340

1941: Dorie Miller, a messman, downs three Japanese planes in the attack on Pearl Harbor.

saturday
7 341

1987: Kurt Schmoke becomes the first African American mayor of Baltimore, Md.

sunday
8 342

ISAAC MURPHY.

December

ISAAC MURPHY

Racing historians call him "the greatest jockey in the history of the sport." Isaac Murphy (1856–1896) dedicated his life to elevating horse racing to an art form. Born January 1, 1861, in Fayette County, Kentucky, Murphy grew up in the saddle—grooming and working the horses in the morning, training and exercising them in the afternoon, and accepting minimal wages for his hard work and dedication.

Murphy won his first race on Glentina at the age of fifteen, and in 1884 he won his first Kentucky Derby on Buchanan, owned by William Bird, an African American. A second Derby victory, on Riley in 1890, and a historic third win, on Kingman in 1891, made him the first jockey to ride winning mounts in the Derby three times and the first to win the prestigious race for two consecutive years. His career record was an incredible 628 wins out of 1,412 starts.

Photograph courtesy
    Library of Congress

s	m	t	w	t	f	s
	1	2	3	4	5	6	7
8	9	10	11	12	13	14
15	16	17	18	19	20	21
22	23	24	25	26	27	28
29	30	31				

DECEMBER

1919: Roy deCarava, first African American photographer to be awarded a Guggenheim Fellowship, is born.

monday

9 343

1950: Dr. Ralph J. Bunche is the first African American to be awarded the Nobel Peace Prize.

tuesday

10 344

1926: Blues singer Willie Mae "Big Mama" Thornton is born in Montgomery, Ala.

wednesday

☽ **11** 345

1995: Willie Brown defeats incumbent mayor Frank Jordan to become the first African American mayor of San Francisco.

thursday

12 346

1957: Daniel A. Chapman becomes Ghana's first ambassador to the United States.

friday

13 347

1963: Dinah Washington, "Queen of the Blues," dies in Detroit, Mich.

saturday

14 348

1883: William A. Hinton, developer of the Hinton test for diagnosing syphilis, is born.

sunday

15 349

DECEMBER

NAT TURNER

Born a slave in Southampton County, Virginia, Nat Turner (1800–1831) was a field hand in the cultivation of cotton and tobacco. His father was a runaway, and so was Nat Turner, who will forever be known for the slave revolt he led in Virginia.

Around 1828, convinced by a vision that he was to lead his people to freedom, he began to lay plans for his rebellion. Beginning in the early morning hours of August 22, 1831, Turner and sixty to eighty other African slaves launched a reign of terror. They killed between fifty-seven and sixty-five whites, beginning with Turner's master's family.

After three days of battle, the state militia managed to suppress the rebellion. Nat Turner was captured on October 31, tried, found guilty, and sentenced to hang. Sixteen of his fellow rebels were also executed.

William Styron wrote a fictionalized account of the revolt in *The Confessions of Nat Turner* (1967).

Courtesy Library of Congress

1976: President Jimmy Carter appoints Andrew Young ambassador to the United Nations.

monday

16 350

1760: Deborah Sampson Gannett, who will disguise herself as a man in order to fight in the Revolutionary War, is born in Plymouth, Va.

tuesday

17 351

1912: Gen. Benjamin O. Davis Sr. is born in Washington, D.C.

wednesday

18 352

1933: Acclaimed actor Cicely Tyson is born in New York City.

thursday

○ **19** 353

1988: Max Robinson, first African American news anchor for a major television network, dies.

friday

20 354

1911: Josh Gibson, Negro Leagues home run king, is born.

saturday

21 355

---

s	m	t	w	t	f	s
1	2	3	4	5	6	7
8	9	10	11	12	13	14
15	16	17	18	19	20	21
22	23	24	25	26	27	28
29	30	31				

DECEMBER

WINTER SOLSTICE 1:15 A.M. (GMT)

1883: Arthur Wergs Mitchell, first African American to be elected to Congress, is born in Lafayette, Ala.

sunday

22 356

DECEMBER

JAMES MEREDITH

James Howard Meredith was born in Kosciusko, Mississippi. After serving in the U.S. Air Force, he found himself in the limelight when he attempted to enroll in the University of Mississippi in 1962—the first African American to make that attempt. White resistance eventually led to rioting that left two dead, and Meredith had to be escorted to classes by the National Guard until he graduated in 1963.

After graduating Meredith continued his defiance; he led a March Against Fear in Mississippi in 1966. The purpose of the march was to encourage blacks to vote. On the second day of the march, a sniper shot Meredith. But he eventually recovered from the wound and completed the march, with Dr. Martin Luther King at his side.

Meredith recounted his experiences in *Three Years in Mississippi*. His most recent book is a history: *Mississippi: A Volume of Eleven Books* (1995).

Photograph courtesy
   Library of Congress

1867: Madam C. J. Walker, first female African American millionaire, is born in Delta, La.

monday
23 357

1853: Author and teacher Octavia Victoria Albert Rogers is born a slave in Oglethorpe, Ga.

tuesday
24 358

CHRISTMAS DAY

1907: Cab Calloway, bandleader and first jazz singer to sell a million records, is born in Rochester, N.Y.

wednesday
25 359

KWANZAA BEGINS
BOXING DAY (CANADA, U.K.)

Kwanzaa begins
Umoja (Unity)
To strive for a principled and harmonious togetherness in the family, community, nation, and world African community.

thursday
26 360

Kujichagulia (Self-Determination)
To define ourselves, name ourselves, create for ourselves, and speak for ourselves.

friday
☾ 27 361

Ujima (Collective Work and Responsibility)
To build and maintain our community together; to make our sisters' and brothers' problems our problems and to solve them together.

saturday
28 362

---

s	m	t	w	t	f	s
1	2	3	4	5	6	7
8	9	10	11	12	13	14
15	16	17	18	19	20	21
22	23	24	25	26	27	28
29	30	31				

DECEMBER

Ujamaa (Cooperative Economics)
To build our own businesses, control the economics of our own communities, and share in all our communities' work and wealth.

sunday
29 363

NANNIE HELEN BURROUGHS

Nannie Helen Burroughs (1879–1961) catapulted onto the political scene with a speech she gave at the National Baptist Convention in 1900 supporting women's rights and strongly condemning mistreatment of women. It was the beginning of a long career as an organizer, religious leader, educator, and political and civil rights activist.

Born in Orange, Virginia, Burroughs later moved with her family to Washington, D.C. There she attended public schools and benefited from the teachings of Mary Church Terrell and her principal, Anna Julia Copper. Burroughs's energy for organizing, her intelligence, and her eloquence in public speaking led her to increasing involvement in movements addressing women's rights, segregation, lynching, employment discrimination, and the disenfranchisement of blacks. At one point her criticisms of the federal government led to her being placed under surveillance.

In 1909, Burroughs founded the National Training School for Women and Girls (later renamed the Nannie Helen Burroughs School), whose motto was "We specialize in the wholly impossible."

Photograph courtesy Library of Congress

s	m	t	w	t	f	s
			1	2	3	4
5	6	7	8	9	10	11
12	13	14	15	16	17	18
19	20	21	22	23	24	25
26	27	28	29	30	31	

JANUARY

Nia (Purpose)
To make our collective vocation the building and development of our community to restore our people to their traditional greatness.

monday
30 364

NEW YEAR'S DAY

Kuumba (Creativity)
To do as much as we can, in whatever way we can, to leave our community more beautiful and beneficial than it was when we inherited it.

tuesday
31 365

Kwanzaa ends
Imani (Faith)
To believe with all our hearts in our people, our parents, our teachers, our leaders, and the righteousness and victory of our struggle.

wednesday
1 1

BANK HOLIDAY (SCOTLAND)

1898: Sadie Tanner Mossell Alexander, first African American to earn a Ph.D. in economics, is born in Philadelphia, Pa.

thursday
● **2** 2

1621: William Tucker is the first African American to be born in America.

friday
3 3

1920: Andrew "Rube" Foster organizes the first black baseball league, the Negro National League.

saturday
4 4

1911: Kappa Alpha Psi Fraternity is chartered as a national organization.

sunday
5 5

2002 INTERNATIONAL HOLIDAYS

Following is a list of major (bank-closing) holidays for some countries around the world. Holidays for the U.S., U.K., and Canada appear on this calendar's grid pages, as well as major Jewish holidays. We apologize if we have omitted countries of interest to you, but space constraints limit our selection.

AUSTRALIA

1	January	New Year's Day
26	January	Australia Day
11	March	Labor Day (Victoria)
29	March	Good Friday
1	April	Easter Monday
25	April	Anzac Day
10	June	Queen's Birthday
5	August	Bank Holiday (New South Wales)
7	October	Labor Day (New South Wales)
5	November	Melbourne Cup Day (Victoria)
25	December	Christmas
26	December	Boxing Day

BRAZIL

1	January	New Year's Day
20	January	Foundation Day (Rio de Janeiro)
25	January	Foundation Day (São Paulo)
11–12	February	Carnival
29	March	Good Friday
21	April	Independence Hero Tiradentes
1	May	Labor Day
30	May	Corpus Christi
9	July	Constitution Day (São Paulo)
7	September	Independence Day
12	October	Religious Day
2	November	All Souls' Day
15	November	Proclamation of the Republic
25	December	Christmas

CHILE

1	January	New Year's Day
29	March	Good Friday
30	March	Holy Saturday
1	May	Labor Day
21	May	Navy Day
30	May	Corpus Christi
29	June	Sts. Peter and Paul
15	August	Assumption Day
2	September	National Unity Day
18	September	Independence Day
19	September	Army Day
12	October	Hispanity Day
1	November	All Saints' Day

8	December	Immaculate Conception
25	December	Christmas
31	December	Bank Holiday

CHINA (see also Hong Kong)

1	January	New Year's Day
12–14	February	Lunar New Year
1–3	May	Labor Day Holiday
1–3	October	National Holiday

DENMARK

1	January	New Year's Day
28	March	Holy Thursday
29	March	Good Friday
1	April	Easter Monday
26	April	General Prayer Day
9	May	Ascension Day
20	May	Whitmonday
5	June	Constitution Day
24	December	Christmas Eve
25	December	Christmas
26	December	Boxing Day

FRANCE

1	January	New Year's Day
1	April	Easter Monday
1	May	Labor Day
8	May	Armistice Day
9	May	Ascension Day
20	May	Whitmonday
14	July	Bastille Day
15	August	Assumption Day
1	November	All Saints' Day
11	November	Armistice Day
25	December	Christmas

GERMANY

1	January	New Year's Day
29	March	Good Friday
1	April	Easter Monday
1	May	Labor Day
9	May	Ascension Day
20	May	Whitmonday
30	May	Corpus Christi
3	October	National Day
24	December	Christmas Eve
25	December	Christmas
26	December	Boxing Day
31	December	New Year's Eve

HONG KONG

1	January	New Year's Day
12–14	February	Lunar New Year

29	March	Good Friday
30	March	Holy Saturday
1	April	Easter Monday
5	April	Ching Ming Festival
1	May	Labor Day
20	May	Buddha's Birthday
15	June	Tuen Ng Day
1	July	SAR Establishment Day
23	September	Mid-Autumn Festival
1	October	National Holiday
14	October	Chung Yeung Day
25–26	Dec.	Christmas Holiday

INDIA

26	January	Republic Day
23	February	Bakr-Id
24	March	Muharram
29	March	Good Friday
1	April	Yearly bank closing
14	April	Babasaheb Ambedkar's Birthday
1	May	Maharashtra Day (or May Day)
24	May	Id-e-Milad (Muhammad's Birthday)
27	May	Buddha Purnima
15	August	Independence Day
21	August	Parsi New Year
30	September	Half-yearly bank closing
2	October	Mahatma Gandhi's Birthday
5	November	Diwali (Laxmipujan)
7	December	Id-ul-Fitar
25	December	Christmas Day (additional holidays to be declared)

ISRAEL

26	February	Purim (Tel Aviv)
27	February	Purim
28	March	First day of Pesach
3	April	Last day of Pesach
17	April	National Independence Day
17	May	Shavuot
18	July	Fast of the Ninth of Av
7–8	September	Rosh Hashanah
15–16	Sept.	Yom Kippur
21	September	First day of Sukkot
28	September	Shemini Atzeret

ITALY

1	January	New Year's Day
6	January	Epiphany

1 April	Easter Monday
25 April	Liberation Day
1 May	Labor Day
15 August	Assumption Day
1 November	All Saints' Day
8 December	Immaculate Conception
25 December	Christmas
26 December	St. Stephen's Day

JAPAN

1–3 January	New Year's Holiday
14 January	Coming of Age Day
11 February	National Foundation Day
21 March	Vernal Equinox
29 April	Greenery Day
3 May	Constitution Day
4 May	National Holiday
6 May	Children's Day
20 July	Ocean Day
16 September	Respect for the Aged Day
23 September	Autumnal Equinox
14 October	Health and Sports Day
4 November	Culture Day
23 November	Labor Thanksgiving Day
23 December	Emperor's Birthday
31 December	New Year's Eve

KENYA

1 January	New Year's Day
29 March	Good Friday
1 April	Easter Monday
1 May	Labor Day
1 June	Madaraka Day
10 October	Moi Day
21 October	Kenyatta Day
6 December	Eid-al-Fitr
12 December	Jamhuri Day
25 December	Christmas
26 December	Boxing Day

KOREA

1 January	New Year's Day
11–13 February	Lunar New Year
1 March	Independence Movement Day
5 April	Arbor Day
1 May	Labor Day
5 May	Children's Day
19 May	Buddha's Birthday
6 June	Memorial Day
17 July	Constitution Day
15 August	Liberation Day
20–22 Sept.	Harvest Moon Festival
3 October	National Foundation Day
25 December	Christmas

MALAYSIA

1 January	New Year's Day
1 February	Federal Territory Day
12–13 February	Lunar New Year
23 February	Hari Raya Haji
15 March	First day of Muharram
1 May	Labor Day
24 May	Prophet Muhammad's Birthday
27 May	Wesak Day
1 June	Yang DiPertuan Agong's Birthday
31 August	National Day
5 November	Deepavali
6–7 December	Hari Raya Puasa
25 December	Christmas

MEXICO

1 January	New Year's Day
5 February	Constitution Day
21 March	Juárez's Birthday
28 March	Holy Thursday
29 March	Good Friday
30 March	Holy Saturday
1 May	Labor Day
5 May	Battle of Puebla
1 September	Government's Report
16 September	Independence Day
20 November	Revolution Day
12 December	Our Lady of Guadalupe
25 December	Christmas

NEW ZEALAND

1–2 January	New Year's Holiday
21 January	Wellington Provincial Anniversary
28 January	Auckland Provincial Anniversary
6 February	Waitangi Day
29 March	Good Friday
1 April	Easter Monday
25 April	Anzac Day
3 June	Queen's Birthday
28 October	Labor Day
25 December	Christmas
26 December	Boxing Day

SAUDI ARABIA

22–26 February	Eid-al-Adha
5–7 December	Eid-al-Fitr
(dates subject to adjustment)	

SINGAPORE

1 January	New Year's Day
12–13 February	Lunar New Year
23 February	Hari Raya Haji

SOUTH AFRICA

29 March	Good Friday
1 May	Labor Day
27 May	Wesak Day
9 August	National Day
5 November	Deepavali
6 December	Hari Raya Puasa
25 December	Christmas

1 January	New Year's Day
21 March	Human Rights Day
29 March	Good Friday
1 April	Family Day
27 April	Freedom Day
1 May	Workers' Day
17 June	Youth Day
9 August	National Women's Day
24 September	Heritage Day
16 December	Day of Reconciliation
25 December	Christmas
26 December	Day of Goodwill

SPAIN

1 January	New Year's Day
6 January	Epiphany
28 March	Holy Thursday
29 March	Good Friday
1 May	Labor Day
2 May	Independence Day
15 May	San Isidro's Day
15 August	Assumption Day
12 October	Hispanity Day
1 November	All Saints' Day
9 November	Our Lady of Almudena
6 December	Constitution Day
8 December	Immaculate Conception
25 December	Christmas

SWITZERLAND

1 January	New Year's Day
2 January	Berchtoldstag
29 March	Good Friday
1 April	Easter Monday
1 May	Labor Day
9 May	Ascension Day
20 May	Whitmonday
1 August	National Day
25 December	Christmas
26 December	St. Stephen's Day
31 December	New Year's Eve

Information courtesy of www.goodbusinessday.com

2003

january

s	m	t	w	t	f	s
			1	2	3	4
5	6	7	8	9	10	11
12	13	14	15	16	17	18
19	20	21	22	23	24	25
26	27	28	29	30	31	

february

s	m	t	w	t	f	s
						1
2	3	4	5	6	7	8
9	10	11	12	13	14	15
16	17	18	19	20	21	22
23	24	25	26	27	28	

march

s	m	t	w	t	f	s
						1
2	3	4	5	6	7	8
9	10	11	12	13	14	15
16	17	18	19	20	21	22
23	24	25	26	27	28	29
30	31					

april

s	m	t	w	t	f	s
		1	2	3	4	5
6	7	8	9	10	11	12
13	14	15	16	17	18	19
20	21	22	23	24	25	26
27	28	29	30			

may

s	m	t	w	t	f	s
				1	2	3
4	5	6	7	8	9	10
11	12	13	14	15	16	17
18	19	20	21	22	23	24
25	26	27	28	29	30	31

june

s	m	t	w	t	f	s
1	2	3	4	5	6	7
8	9	10	11	12	13	14
15	16	17	18	19	20	21
22	23	24	25	26	27	28
29	30					

july

s	m	t	w	t	f	s
		1	2	3	4	5
6	7	8	9	10	11	12
13	14	15	16	17	18	19
20	21	22	23	24	25	26
27	28	29	30	31		

august

s	m	t	w	t	f	s
					1	2
3	4	5	6	7	8	9
10	11	12	13	14	15	16
17	18	19	20	21	22	23
24	25	26	27	28	29	30
31						

september

s	m	t	w	t	f	s
	1	2	3	4	5	6
7	8	9	10	11	12	13
14	15	16	17	18	19	20
21	22	23	24	25	26	27
28	29	30				

october

s	m	t	w	t	f	s
			1	2	3	4
5	6	7	8	9	10	11
12	13	14	15	16	17	18
19	20	21	22	23	24	25
26	27	28	29	30	31	

november

s	m	t	w	t	f	s
						1
2	3	4	5	6	7	8
9	10	11	12	13	14	15
16	17	18	19	20	21	22
23	24	25	26	27	28	29
30						

december

s	m	t	w	t	f	s
	1	2	3	4	5	6
7	8	9	10	11	12	13
14	15	16	17	18	19	20
21	22	23	24	25	26	27
28	29	30	31			